No Fluff, Just Stuff Anthology

The 2006 Edition

No Fluff, Just Stuff Anthology

The 2006 Edition

Neal Ford, Editor

with Scott Davis
David Geary
Andrew Glover
Stuart Halloway
Kirk Knoernschild
Mark Richards
Jared Richardson
Ian Roughley
Brian Sletten
Venkat Subramaniam
Eitan Suez
Glenn Vanderburg

The Pragmatic Bookshelf
Raleigh, North Carolina   Dallas, Texas

Many of the designations used by manufacturers and sellers to distinguish their products are claimed as trademarks. Where those designations appear in this book, and The Pragmatic Programmers, LLC was aware of a trademark claim, the designations have been printed in initial capital letters or in all capitals. The Pragmatic Starter Kit, The Pragmatic Programmer, Pragmatic Programming, Pragmatic Bookshelf and the linking *g* device are trademarks of The Pragmatic Programmers, LLC.

Every precaution was taken in the preparation of this book. However, the publisher assumes no responsibility for errors or omissions, or for damages that may result from the use of information (including program listings) contained herein.

Our Pragmatic courses, workshops, and other products can help you and your team create better software and have more fun. For more information, as well as the latest Pragmatic titles, please visit us at

http://www.pragmaticprogrammer.com

ISBN 0-97761666-5

Printed on acid-free paper with 85% recycled, 30% post-consumer content.

First printing, June 2006

Version: 2006-5-8

Contents

No Fluff Just Stuff.com

Greetings!

This NFJS anthology exists for two reasons. We wanted to provide you with interesting and informational articles, and we also wanted to give you an indication of the quality of the speakers we have on the NFJS tour. NFJS takes great pride in featuring some of the premier technical speaking talent in the country. The majority of our speakers are also accomplished authors.

For those of you not familiar with the No Fluff, Just Stuff Symposium Series, our beginnings can be traced back to 2001 in Boulder, Colorado. Since that time, we have organized more than 75 symposia throughout the United States and Canada with more than 12,000 attendees. Our success has been a result of focusing on high-quality technical presentations, great speakers, limited attendance (capped at 250 people) and no "marketecture." As a result of the NFJS symposium tour success, the next step in our evolutionary process is to begin publishing a yearly anthology by our speakers/authors that compliments the sessions they give in 2006. I know you will enjoy the chapters within this anthology, and I hope you will join us at an NFJS tour stop if you have not done so already. Thank you in advance for your support and patronage.

A special thanks to Libby, Zachary, and Hannah. All three of you have embraced the vision of No Fluff, Just Stuff from the beginning through your efforts and your belief in me. I love you all!

All the best,

Jay Zimmerman
NFJS Symposium Creator & Director

http://www.nofluffjuststuff.com

Preface

About two years ago, I participated in an event that changed my life, although I didn't quite grasp the significance of it at the time: I spoke at my first No Fluff, Just Stuff conference in Austin, Texas. My publisher, Manning, put me in touch with Jay Zimmerman, and we played phone tag for a few weeks. When I finally talked to him about speaking at that first show, he kept going on and on that "this show is more advanced than other conferences" and "I'm really dedicated to keep the quality sky high." Basically, this was the same stuff I'd heard over and over again from other conference organizers. I was no spring chicken at conference speaking. I had already presented more than 100 conference sessions all over the world. So, I thought "Yada, yada, more of the 'we're better than everyone else' blather."

But a funny thing happened in Austin: he was right! Suddenly, my ace game was barely adequate. I distinctly remember telling co-workers when I returned that I felt like a kid eating at the adult's table. Jay had (and has) managed to create an extraordinary gathering in every city he visits. Maybe it's the weekend seclusion, or the longer than average sessions, or the high level of discourse in the sessions that spills into the hallways and the meals. Maybe it's everyone you meet. It's all those things, with one more keystone ingredient: the speakers. I am honored and humbled to be considered a part of this extraordinary group of individuals: the most brilliant minds in the industry, genuinely personable, gregarious, funny, and centered. Jay has created a work of genius, gathering this group to talk about technology 27 weekends a year.

Back in the 1920s, a group of writers, actors, and other artists started gathering a few times a week at the Algonquin Hotel restaurant. This group included Dorothy Parker and Harpo Marx, among others (for a great movie that depicts this group and era, check out *Mrs. Parker and the Vicious Circle*). According to legend, the Algonquin Round Table discussions were the wittiest in history because they attracted the quickest, most sarcastic people in New York at that time, who were the best in the world. Here are a few samples:

- Robert Sherwood, reviewing cowboy hero Tom Mix: "They say he rides as if he's part of the horse, but they don't say which part."

- Dorothy Parker: "That woman speaks 18 languages and can't say 'no' in any of them."

- George S. Kaufman: Once when asked by a press agent, "How do I get my leading lady's name into your newspaper?" Kaufman replied, "Shoot her."

No Fluff has created a geek version of this same phenomenon: the speakers' dinner. On Saturday night, the speakers go somewhere and eat, and every one of those gatherings ends up being the most fascinating conversation you can imagine. All these brilliant people, gather to talk about the topics they've been thinking about all week that they can't discuss with their spouses. I've probably had more revelations over food during the last two years than I've had my entire life prior to the speakers' dinner. No Fluff created for the speakers a computer science version of the Algonquin Round Table (at a Cheesecake Factory in your neighborhood).

Until now, no one other than the speakers had access to this fascinating and varied stream of conversation. Last year, Jay approached me with the idea of creating an annual book, featuring articles by some of the speakers and covering the topics about which they are passionate. That's when the idea (but not the name) of the anthology arose. I agreed to edit it, if for no other reason than to be the first to get to read all the chapters. We talked about it over the winter, set up deadlines, contacted the speakers, and waited on chapters. When they started arriving, I saw that Jay was right: we had a fascinating, diverse, engaging set of chapters, whose only common characteristics were No Fluff, Just Stuff and technical acumen.

Giving this beast a title was the only chore left. When I was a young boy, I was a voracious reader of science fiction. My favorite books were the anthologies: *Hugo Award Winners for 1970* and *The Best New Sci Fi & Fantasy, 1973*. What I liked most about these books was the sense of anticipation for every story. Because each story had a different author, the styles of the stories ranged far and wide. Thus, the name *No Fluff, Just Stuff Anthology: The 2006 Edition* was born.

Just like those hoary old science fiction anthologies, each chapter in this book is wildly different, both in style and in topic. Whether you read it from cover to cover or just jump right into the middle, you will be pleasantly surprised. This book is the next best thing to a dinner invitation at No Fluff, Just Stuff in all 27 cities. *Bon appetit!*

Neal Ford
April, 2006

Chapter 1

Real-World Web Services

by Scott Davis

Scott Davis is a senior software engineer at OpenLogic. He is passionate about open source solutions and agile development. He has worked on a variety of Java platforms, from J2EE to J2SE to J2ME (sometimes all on the same project).

He is the coauthor of JBoss at Work [MD05], quite possibly the world's first agile J2EE book. He is also responsible for Google Maps API: Adding Where to Your Application[1] and the forthcoming Pragmatic GIS [Dav06].

Scott is a frequent presenter at national conferences (such as No Fluff, Just Stuff) and local user groups. He was the president of the Denver Java Users Group in 2003 when it was voted one of the top-ten JUGs in North America. After a quick move north, he is currently active in the leadership of the Boulder Java Users Group. Keep up with him at http://www.davisworld.org.

Scott's list of favorite books and tools starts on page 215.

---

[1] *http://www.pragmaticprogrammer.com/titles/sdgmapi*

Ajax

SOA

When software historians reflect on the first decade of the 21st century, they will most likely remembered it as the time when years-old technologies were held up as recent innovations. Just as Ajax (Asynchronous JavaScript And XML) is based primarily on the XMLHttpRequest object that was incorporated into web browsers during the late 1990s, the current infatuation with the notion of SOA has prompted many curmudgeons to dub it Same Old Architecture instead of Service-Oriented Architecture.

In its defense, SOA is worth reevaluating. Given the meteoric rise in popularity of the Internet, this might be the "perfect storm" of technologies and philosophies that finally moves SOA from theory to business reality.

In order to implement SOA in your organization, you are forced to run a gauntlet of loosely defined and poorly understood TLAs (three-letter acronyms)—SOAP and WSDL, REST, and POX, to name just a few. Compounding matters, as developers we often rush to an implementation without fully understanding the semantics behind it. In this chapter, we'll discuss the philosophy of SOA. You can take two very different roads on the way to SOA. Both will eventually get you to the same destination, but they take distinctly different routes.

To begin our journey, let's put a more concrete definition together for SOA.

1.1 What Is SOA?

We defined SOA earlier as Service-Oriented Architecture, but what does that really mean? The Wikipedia entry says, "Unlike traditional point-to-point architectures, SOAs comprise loosely coupled, highly interoperable application services."[2]

"Services" refers to simple stateless resources that can be accessed remotely, perhaps getStockQuote('IBM') or getCurrentTemp('Denver'). These services can return either a single data value or a complex document.

"Loosely coupled, highly interoperable" echoes a common sentiment used to describe technologies related to the Internet. Several books use variations of this theme in their titles, such as *Small Pieces Loosely Joined: A Unified Theory of the Web* [Wei02] by David Weinberger and

---

[2]http://en.wikipedia.org/wiki/Service-oriented_architecture

Loosely Coupled: The Missing Pieces of Web Services [Kay03] by Doug Kaye. The success of the Internet is due largely to its insistence on platform-, language-, and vendor-neutral solutions. Interoperability is demonstrated every second of every day as Windows, Linux, and Mac servers and clients seamlessly interact with each other in as many different programming languages as there are spoken languages.

So is WS (web services) synonymous with SOA? Wikipedia goes on to say, "Most definitions of SOA identify the use of web services (i.e., using SOAP or REST) in its implementation. However, one can implement SOA using any service-based technology." To prove this, one needs to look only as far as the modernization of the lowly parking meter. From Florida to Las Vegas to California, examples are popping up all over the place of a cell phone/parking meter interface. Rather than fumble around for loose change, the driver calls a number posted on the parking meter or sends an SMS message. When the meter is about to expire, it sends a message to the phone, giving the driver a chance to add more time without having to physically visit the meter again. This service would not be possible if the technology surrounding it wasn't ubiquitous. (Imagine seeing a sign that read, "This meter works best with T-Mobile phones. Verizon subscribers should park down the block.")

An SOA can be implemented using a wide variety of protocols (SMTP, XMPP, or SNMP, to name a few), although HTTP is by far the most common of the bunch.

1.2   What Is a WS?

A web service is a remote, message-oriented type of SOA that rides atop HTTP. In simple terms, this means you can make a request over port 80 and get an XML response. Of course, the type of HTTP request you make (GET, POST, PUT, DELETE), the format of the request, and the format of the response can all vary from WS implementation to implementation. But before we get into the details of the various implementations, let's spend a bit more time deconstructing the name web services.

When they think of the World Wide Web, most people think of viewing web pages in a web browser. As developers, we can take this one step further and see it as making a GET request over HTTP and receiving an HTML response.

HTTP, despite the name Hypertext Transport Protocol, doesn't much care what the datatype of its payload is. Every HTTP response includes a MIME type. For web pages, the MIME type is generally text/html or application/xhtml+xml. For images, the MIME type can be image/png, image/jpeg, or image/gif depending on the file format. So as you can see, sending XML back (text/xml) isn't asking HTTP to do anything out of the ordinary.[3]

So if HTTP doesn't care whether it's returning XML instead of HTML, why did the W3C take great pains to differentiate web services from the plain old Web that even your grandmother understands? The simple answer is *intent*.

The plain old Web that we've known and loved for the past 15 years is based on presenting data to you in an appealing manner. Whether you're using simple physical markup tags such as bold, italic, and (grimace) blink or using sophisticated CSS (Cascading Style Sheets), the whole point of the exercise is to affect the appearance of the data:

```
<h1>Honda Accord</h1>
<b>Color:</b> Black<br/>
<b>Sunroof:</b> Yes<br/>
```

Web services are not concerned about the appearance of the data at all. The goal of WS is to leverage the ubiquity of the Web to get you the unadorned data. It is the responsibility of the WS consumer to format the data in an appropriate way:

```
<car type="Honda Accord">
  <color>Black</color>
  <sunroof>Yes</sunroof>
</car>
```

If you think about it in terms of MVC (Model, View, Controller pattern), HTML is the view; XML is the model.

Almost all of the major websites have WS APIs that allow you to get at the data without having to dig it out of the HTML. eBay handles more than a billion WS requests a month, accounting for nearly half of its entire business.[4]

---

[3]For a list of all registered MIME types, see http://www.iana.org/assignments/media-types/ or the file mime.types in the conf/ directory of your friendly neighborhood Apache web server.

[4]See http://developer.ebay.com/join/whitepapers/webservicesinaction for more details.

In the physical world, why do most cities have bus, taxi, and limo services? Why do only a select few have subways, trolleys, monorails, or gondolas? The obvious answer is infrastructure; the former services can take advantage of the existing city streets, while the latter services require expensive, specialized, proprietary platforms. In software terms, what does WS have going for it that other remoting (RMI, DCOM, CORBA) and messaging (JMS, MSMQ) architectures don't? The answer is that nearly every company has an Internet connection, a web server, and port 80 open on its firewall.

1.3 What Is SOAP?

SOAP initially stood for Simple Object Access Protocol, but like many other technology-related acronyms (JDBC comes to mind), this one is now officially just a collection of four letters that has no deeper significance. SOAP and its sibling WSDL (Web Services Description Language) comprise arguably the most popular form of WS.[5]

SOAP

WSDL

SOAP requests and responses are well-formed XML documents. SOAP messages have a standard envelope that contains a header and a body. Just like a letter in the physical world, the envelope has an address that allows a customizable payload (the body) to be delivered to the recipient.

The WSDL document provides everything necessary to complete a SOAP transaction: the URL of the WS provider, the names of the services and any arguments, and the exact format of both the SOAP request and the response bodies. Although the WSDL isn't exactly an easy read for humans, it is expressed in a standard XML format. This means a number of utilities exist that can automatically create a SOAP client without any human intervention.

To see SOAP in action, let's look to the venerable search engine Google.[6] No one needs a tutorial explaining how to use the web interface—you type in your search criteria, click the search button, and get a list of results in HTML, as shown in Figure 1.1, on the next page.

But what if you want to get the results back as XML instead of HTML? The first step is to download the free Google web API toolkit.[7] The

---

[5]See http://www.w3.org/TR/soap/ for the full specification.

[6]http://www.google.com

[7]http://www.google.com/apis

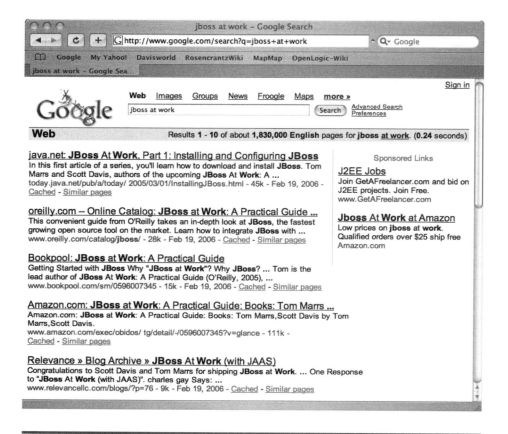

Figure 1.1: SEARCH RESULTS FROM THE GOOGLE WEBSITE

toolkit contains a WSDL document describing the interface, examples of SOAP requests and responses, and sample code in several programming languages showing you how to make the requests and manipulate the responses. You'll also need to register for a free API key that must accompany each WS request.

To perform the same query using SOAP, you need to construct a SOAP request, like the one in Figure 1.2, on the facing page. You use HTTP POST to send the request to the service. The SOAP response comes back as XML. (See Figure 1.3, on the next page, for a snippet.) Once you have the results, you can use any standard XML toolkit (JDOM, Castor, XMLBeans, etc.) to transform the output into the format of your choice.

```
1   <?xml version='1.0' encoding='UTF-8'?>
2
3   <SOAP-ENV:Envelope
4       xmlns:SOAP-ENV="http://schemas.xmlsoap.org/soap/envelope/"
5       xmlns:xsi="http://www.w3.org/1999/XMLSchema-instance"
6       xmlns:xsd="http://www.w3.org/1999/XMLSchema">
7     <SOAP-ENV:Body>
8       <ns1:doGoogleSearch
9           xmlns:ns1="urn:GoogleSearch"
10          SOAP-ENV:encodingStyle="http://schemas.xmlsoap.org/soap/encoding/">
11        <key xsi:type="xsd:string">00000000000000000000000000000000</key>
12        <q xsi:type="xsd:string">jboss at work</q>
13        <start xsi:type="xsd:int">0</start>
14        <maxResults xsi:type="xsd:int">10</maxResults>
15        <filter xsi:type="xsd:boolean">true</filter>
16        <restrict xsi:type="xsd:string"></restrict>
17        <safeSearch xsi:type="xsd:boolean">false</safeSearch>
18        <lr xsi:type="xsd:string"></lr>
19        <ie xsi:type="xsd:string">latin1</ie>
20        <oe xsi:type="xsd:string">latin1</oe>
21      </ns1:doGoogleSearch>
22    </SOAP-ENV:Body>
23  </SOAP-ENV:Envelope>
```

Figure 1.2: A GOOGLE SOAP REQUEST

```
12            <item xsi:type="ns1:ResultElement">
13              <cachedSize xsi:type="xsd:string">12k</cachedSize>
14              <hostName xsi:type="xsd:string"></hostName>
15              <snippet xsi:type="xsd:string">In this first article of a series, you'll learn how
.   to download and install JBoss. Tom Marrs and Scott Davis, authors of the upcoming JBoss At
.   Work: A ...</snippet>
16              <directoryCategory xsi:type="ns1:DirectoryCategory">
17                <specialEncoding xsi:type="xsd:string"></specialEncoding>
18                <fullViewableName xsi:type="xsd:string"></fullViewableName>
19              </directoryCategory>
20              <relatedInformationPresent xsi:type="xsd:boolean">true</relatedInformationPresent>
21              <directoryTitle xsi:type="xsd:string"></directoryTitle>
22              <summary xsi:type="xsd:string"></summary>
23              <URL xsi:type="xsd:string">http://today.java.net/pub/a/today/2005/03/01/
.   InstallingJBoss.html</URL>
24              <title xsi:type="xsd:string">&lt;b&gt;JBoss At Work&lt;/b&gt;</title>
25            </item>
```

Figure 1.3: A PORTION OF A GOOGLE SOAP RESPONSE

The Apache Axis project[8] is an open source SOAP framework. In addition to giving you the capability to host your own SOAP-based WS, it provides tools to seamlessly create SOAP clients as well. WSDL2Java and Java2WSDL, as the names suggest, allow you to generate Java clients from a WSDL document.

Maven[9] takes this one step further. If you provide a URL to a WSDL document, Maven will download it from the Web and build a full Java client including unit tests. Several chapters in *Maven: A Developer's Notebook* [MO05] by Vincent Massol and Timothy M. O'Brien discuss this process in great detail.

Implementing your SOA in SOAP has many benefits. SOAP is a mature, well-understood specification with a robust ecosystem of supporting toolsets. Although requests are most often sent over HTTP, native bindings for other transports are supported as well.

However, SOAP is not without its drawbacks. As you saw, it is quite verbose; few people will tackle SOAP without a toolkit to autogenerate the lion's share of the requisite code infrastructure. This has led a vocal minority to say, "SOAP is the EJB of the XML world"—meaning it's undeniably powerful but perhaps heavier-weight than many solutions require. It's like using a sledgehammer as a flyswatter.

Another common complaint is that SOAP isn't particularly browser-friendly. JavaScript doesn't have robust XML support, making SOAP requests possible but not exactly trivial. These complaints have given rise to a "kinder, gentler" form of WS: REST.

1.4 What Is REST?

REST

REST is short for Representational State Transfer. Behind that relatively complicated sounding name is a simple concept: if you want to access a service over the Web, why not use a simple web URL? Provided it returns XML, a request such as

```
http://www.someservice.com/store?action=getCarList&amp;make=Honda
```

is every bit the web service that SOAP is.

---

[8]http://ws.apache.org/axis/
[9]http://maven.apache.org/

```
- <ResultSet xsi:schemaLocation="urn:yahoo:srch http://api.search.yahoo.com/WebSearchServ:
  - <Result>
    - <Title>
        Amazon.com: JBoss at Work: A Practical Guide: Books
      </Title>
    - <Summary>
        Amazon.com: JBoss at Work: A Practical Guide: Books by Tom Marrs,Scott Davis ... v
      </Summary>
    - <Url>
        http://www.amazon.com/exec/obidos/tg/detail/-/0596007345?v=glance
      </Url>
    - <ClickUrl>
        http://uk.wrs.yahoo.com/_ylt=A9htfSGYz_pDVWAATqDdmMwF;_ylu=X3oDMTB c
      </ClickUrl>
      <ModificationDate>1137312000</ModificationDate>
      <MimeType>text/html</MimeType>
    - <Cache>
      - <Url>
          http://uk.wrs.yahoo.com/_ylt=A9htfSGYz_pDVWAAU6DdmMwF;_ylu=X3oDMT
        </Url>
        <Size>112159</Size>
      </Cache>
  </Result>
```

Figure 1.4: SEARCH RESULTS FROM THE YAHOO WS API

REST was formally introduced in the 2000 doctoral dissertation of Roy Fielding,[10] but the idea was woven into the fabric of the Web from the beginning. Every resource on the Internet has a unique identifier—a URI (Uniform Resource Identifier). The term URL (Uniform Resource Locator) is a type of URI that in addition to identifying a service also describes how to locate it.

URI
URL

The popular definition of a RESTful WS is anything that accepts a simple HTTP GET request instead of a formal SOAP request. In practice, many of these URLs bear only a superficial resemblance to Fielding's original definition of REST (including the example URL I presented earlier). After we examine a popular RESTful WS, I'll give an example of a canonical one.

In contrast to Google's SOAP-based WS API, Yahoo[11] offers a RESTful API for searching. To download the sample SDK and register for a free API key, visit http://developer.yahoo.net/.

Once you have a key, you can make a RESTful request by putting together a simple URL (shown here split onto two lines):

---

[10]http://www.ics.uci.edu/~fielding/pubs/dissertation/top.htm
[11]http://www.yahoo.com

```
http://api.search.yahoo.com/WebSearchService/V1/webSearch?
     appid=00000000&amp;query=jboss+at+work
```

If you type this URL into a web browser, you can easily see the results, as shown in Figure 1.4, on the preceding page. Of course, a real application would take these results and transform them into something more interesting than raw XML.

Yahoo offers a number of RESTful web services, in addition to search, ranging from stock quotes to shopping to weather forecasts. Each service is a breeze to play with—construct a slightly different URL, and you're off to the races.

Many companies offer both SOAP and REST interfaces. Notably, Amazon reports an almost nine to one preference among developers for its RESTful interface based on traffic patterns.[12]

Opponents of REST argue that it lacks a formal mechanism for defining the interface and response format like WSDL, which in turn means that there isn't a Maven-like way to magically create clients. Supporters of REST point to examples such as Amazon, suggesting that the interface is so easy to learn that it doesn't require a client generator. Any tool or library that supports web requests (HttpClient, wget, curl) is already REST-enabled.

POJO

POX

Just as the term POJO (Plain Old Java Object) is often used to contrast more complicated, formal frameworks such as EJB, POX (Plain Old XML) is gaining popularity when characterizing RESTful web services.

RPC

Even though the two search engine giants offer WS APIs that use distinct syntaxes, Fielding would probably argue that they are more similar than different. Both are essentially RPC (Remote Procedure Call) interfaces. A true RESTful WS is resource-centric, not RPC-centric.

Consider the following URL:

```
http://www.somestore.com/books/jboss_at_work
```

In a RESTful system, making an HTTP GET request to that URI returns the XML *representation* of that resource. If you want to get a different book, you make a different request:

```
http://www.somestore.com/books/pragmatic_gis
```

---

[12]Visit http://www.amazon.com/gp/browse.html/002-7648597-5380869?node=3435361 to download the SDK and register for a free API key.

If you want a list of all books, you ask for the following:

```
http://www.somestore.com/books
```

If instead you want a list of DVDs, you ask for the following:

```
http://www.somestore.com/dvds
```

Doesn't that seem like a natural way to interact with a WS?

In an RPC interface, the emphasis is on defining unique method names, for instance getBook('JBoss at Work'), addBook('JBoss at Work'), and delete-Book('JBoss at Work'). It is a method-centric worldview, where you must pass in the unique identifier.

When you look at the world through resource-centric glasses, it is the object that is a first-class citizen, not the method. You perform actions on objects rather than passing the object to an action.

To continue exploring our hypothetical RESTful interface, I would use HTTP POST to insert a new book:

```
http://www.somestore.com/books/some_new_title
```

An HTTP DELETE would delete the book. An HTTP PUT would update the resource. For a great set of articles on creating your own RESTful API, see Joe Gregorio's series on XML.com.[13]

To see a real-world example of this, consider the blogosphere. The URI of my weblog is http://www.davisworld.org/blojsom/blog. There's a bit of implementation bleed-through—I use Blojsom[14] for my blogging software—but the point remains valid nonetheless. If you want to visit my blog, you can visit that URL.

I am the only person blogging at that address right now, but Blojsom supports multiple users. If you want to see an individual's blog, you simply expand the URI a bit: http://www.davisworld.org/blojsom/blog/scott. (Since I am the only user at that URI, the real URI is as follows:

```
http://www.davisworld.org/blojsom/blog/default
```

Visiting that URL will always give you the latest list of blog entries. If you want to go to a specific blog entry, you can expand the URI a bit further:

```
http://www.davisworld.org/blojsom/blog/default/2006/02/01/Evolve.html
```

---

[13]http://www.xml.com/pub/at/34
[14]http://blojsom.sf.net/

permalink

By deconstructing the permalink, you can see how Blojsom organizes its entries: first by user, then by year, then by month, then by day, and finally by title. If you shorten the URL a bit to

```
http://www.davisworld.org/blojsom/blog/default/2006/02
```

Blojsom will return all entries that were posted in February 2006.

The Atom Syndication Format and Atom Publishing Protocol RFCs further define the rest of the RESTful nature of the blogosphere—providing ways of publishing new entries, deleting entries, etc. (RSS is another blog syndication API, but it is a more RPC-like implementation.) The ROME toolkit[15] is a Java API that allows you to programmatically interact with both Atom and RSS feeds.

1.5 What Is JSON?

JSON

Because XML results are still problematic to parse using JavaScript, regardless of the request format used, a third alternative for WS is gaining steam with the Ajax crowd. JSON (JavaScript Object Notation) based web services return data in JavaScript instead of XML.

Despite the word JavaScript in the title, there are JSON bindings for more than 15 different languages, including Java.[16]

At first glance, JSON seems to simply swap out angle braces in favor of curly braces, commas, and colons. But by expressing the data structures in a more JavaScript-friendly manner, you can simply eval() the returned data, getting well-formed JavaScript objects out the other side.

To see JSON in action, let's revisit the Yahoo API.

By appending output=json to the end of our query, we get a very different-looking set of results:

```
{"Title":"java.net: JBoss at Work, Part 1: Installing and Configuring JBoss",
"Summary":"In this first article of a series ...",
"Url":"http:\/\/today.java.net\/pub\/a\/today\/2005\/03\/01\/Ins...",
"ClickUrl":"http:\/\/today.java.net\/pub\/a\/today\/2005\/03\/01...",
"ModificationDate":1140076800,
"MimeType":"text\/html",
"Cache":{"Url":"http:...","Size":"45524"}},
```

---

[15]https://rome.dev.java.net/

[16]See http://www.json.org/ for more information.

Ruby aficionados use a similar format, YAML, as the default serialization syntax. Early in its life, YAML meant Yet Another Markup Language. Recently, that definition has been updated to YAML Ain't Markup Language. YAML parsers exist in a number of different languages other than Ruby, including Java. *YAML*

Software developers are a pragmatic bunch—if XML support continues to lag in their language of choice (especially in something as widespread as JavaScript), expect to see more web services popping up that cater to their immediate needs. If WS providers have to choose between historical precedence and immediate market share, which do you think they'll select?

Of course, as request and response formats multiply, that will bring a new set of challenges for the software developer to tackle. A whole new class of software is emerging based on the notion of ESB (Enterprise Service Bus). An ESB toolkit such as ServiceMix[17] allows you to normalize queries across multiple disparate services using generalized XML syntaxes such as BPEL (Business Process Execution Language) and the new JBI (Java Business Interface) API. *ESB* *BPEL* *JBI*

Regardless of which new languages and protocols emerge in the future to support SOAs, rest assured that there will be some old wizened developer in the background muttering under his breath, "SOAs? Why are these young whippersnappers getting so excited about SOAs? I've been doing the same thing for years...."

---

[17] http://servicemix.org/

Chapter 2

DSLs and Language-Oriented Programming

by Neal Ford

Neal Ford is an application architect at ThoughtWorks, a global IT consultancy with an exclusive focus on end-to-end software development and delivery. He is the designer and developer of applications, instructional materials, magazine articles, and video presentations and author of the books Developing with Delphi: Object-Oriented Techniques [WFW95], JBuilder 3 Unleashed [FWA$^+$99], and Art of Java Web Development [For03]. His language proficiencies include Java, C#/.NET, Ruby, Object Pascal, C++, and C. His primary consulting focus is the building of large-scale enterprise applications. Neal has taught on-site classes nationally and internationally to all branches of the military and to many Fortune 500 companies. He is also an internationally acclaimed speaker, having spoken at numerous developer conferences worldwide. If you have an insatiable curiosity about Neal, visit his website at http://www.nealford.com. He welcomes feedback and can be reached at mailto:nford@thoughtworks.com.

Neal's book and tool selections start on page 216.

Have you ever wondered why you spend more time writing XML than Java? XML seems to have taken over development in Java (and other languages). Another interesting (and related) question is this: why is everyone and his brother talking about Ruby and Ruby on Rails all of a sudden? And finally, is there an evolutionary step beyond object-oriented programming?

This chapter addresses these and other questions. It is about building domain-specific languages using Java and a new development discipline called language-oriented programming, which is a style of programming where you create your own language keyed to a particular problem domain. Before I get into all *that*, though, I want to talk about why on Earth you would want to do this.

language-oriented programming

2.1 The Motivation for Domain-Specific Languages

dynamic language

A dynamic language (or dynamically typed language) doesn't require type safety. In other words, if you have a variable that currently holds an int, you can assign a String to it with no complaints. Most dynamic languages don't require you to specify a type for a variable—variables hold whatever you give them. Ruby proponents call this *duck typing*:: if the variable responds to a message that asks it to quack like a duck and it quacks, it must be a duck. This is clearly different from the way that Java (and other strongly typed languages) work, where each variable represents a certain type. Examples of dynamic languages include JavaScript, Lisp, Smalltalk, Python, and Ruby.

If you look at the way experienced developers use dynamic languages, you see a pattern emerge. Instead of modeling the problem using objects or some other structural approach, they tend to write a new language to solve the problem. This language is domain-specific, meaning that it represents high-level abstractions of the problem domain. Using DSLs to solve problems is well stated in Eric Raymond's *Art of UNIX Programming* [Ray03] in Section 1.6.14:

"Avoid hand-hacking: write programs to write programs when you can."

little languages

Raymond is talking about the Unix tradition of little languages, which are small, specific languages used to solve a single problem.

A couple of examples will help me make my case. In the book *Hackers and Painters* [Gra04], Paul Graham describes the first "build your own" ecommerce solution (which was eventually sold to Yahoo Stores). The application, written in Lisp as a DSL, closely modeled the problem of building an ecommerce store. Their competitors at the time wrote their applications in C. Paul's group wrote their application in their DSL on top of Lisp, which closely modeled the problem domain of building on-line stores. Because Paul's group operated at a much higher level of abstraction (i.e., away from low-level Lisp syntax), they responded to change more quickly. When their competitors added a new feature, they could mimic that feature within days. When Paul's team added new features, it took their competitors weeks to match them. The approach of modeling the problem as a DSL created a significant advantage.

Another example of a clever use of a domain-specific language is Ruby on Rails, the web framework and persistence library written in Ruby. Ruby on Rails is popular because it is extraordinarily productive for some classes of web application development. Users of Ruby on Rails are exuberant to the point of annoyance: they keep talking about what a joy it is to use. The reason for its productivity and popularity revolves around how it is written. Ruby on Rails is a DSL designed for building web applications that feature persistence. Developers who blissfully use it operate at a higher level of abstraction than those using a Java framework.

2.2 Some Definitions

I first started talking about building domain-specific languages at No Fluff, Just Stuff in March 2005. The genesis for the idea was the observation of the way developers used languages such as Ruby. Then, about six months later, Martin Fowler (Chief Scientist at *Thought*Works) wrote an article about DSLs entitled "Language Workbenches: The Killer App for Domain-Specific Languages?" It turns out that Martin talked about the same stuff I was talking about, but he applied his uncanny ability of assigning nomenclature to the problem. Without realizing it, he added sorely lacking definitions to what I had been talking about all along. After getting his permission, I adopted his definitions to organize what I was talking about, and I use those definitions here.

Nomenclature

A domain-specific language is a limited form of computer language designed for a specific class of problems. In most of the existing literature, when authors refer to DSLs, it is always about a problem domain, not boundary classes. When talking about model objects in

domain-specific language

entity

boundary

an application, you can separate them by function into either an entity or a boundary class. The entities model the problem domain and generally contain just data fields and business rules. Boundary classes handle the transitions between the layers of the application. Examples of boundary classes include database access, user interface, service, and any other class used to facilitate the building of the application's model. The entities represent *why* you build the application, and the boundaries represent *how* you build it. In the existing literature, DSLs mostly represent entities. In my view, you can use a DSL for any type of limited problem domain that encompasses entities and boundaries. Ruby on Rails addresses this boundary neighborhood, with support for persistence and user interfaces.

Language-oriented programming

Language-oriented programming describes the general style of development that operates around the idea of building software around a set of domain-specific languages. This is an evolutionary step beyond object-oriented programming because the building blocks of your DSL (if you are writing it on top of Java) are classes, objects, aspects, and all the other weapons you already have in your arsenal. This isn't about replacing object-oriented programming; it's about operating at a higher level of abstraction. The new language you create encapsulates your problem domain, and the new language in turn is written using Java features and extensions as its building blocks.

Types of DSLs

internal DSL

Rake

Two types of DSLs exist: internal and external. An internal DSL is a domain-specific language written "on top" of the underlying syntax of your base language. If Java is your base language, then an internal DSL written in Java uses Java syntax to define the language. Most of the DSLs that exist today are internal DSLs: Ruby on Rails, the example from *Hackers and Painters*, and Rake (the Ruby make utility). Programming languages with forgiving syntax (like Lisp, Smalltalk, Python, and Ruby) have spawned DSLs for obvious reasons: the looser the syntax rules, the easier it is to create a new language on top of it.

2.3 DSLs Underfoot

Whether you realize it or not, you've been using DSLs for years. You haven't noticed them because they have always been hidden, either in regular, mundane code or in XML documents. Here are two examples.

J2EE Front Controller in Web Frameworks

Virtually every web framework in the Java world uses the J2EE Front
Controller design pattern. This pattern is generally implemented using
a servlet that intercepts requests to your web application and dis-
patches control to a workflow component (for example, an Action class
in Struts or a Handler class in JavaServer Faces).

Each of the implementations of this pattern follow the same general
structure. They all have some framework classes, used to establish *framework*
scaffolding. This example shows a simple implementation of this pattern. This is the base class for the workflow classes, Action:

`code/neal/paramcmd/pc/Action.java`

```java
abstract public class Action {
    private HttpServletRequest request;
    private HttpServletResponse response;
    private ServletContext servletContext;

    abstract public void execute();

    public void forward(String forwardResource) {
        try {
            RequestDispatcher rd =
                getRequest().getRequestDispatcher(
                forwardResource);
            rd.forward(getRequest(), getResponse());
        } catch (IOException iox) {
            servletContext.log("Forward Error", iox);
        } catch (ServletException sx) {
            servletContext.log("Servlet Error", sx);
        }
    }

    public void setRequest(HttpServletRequest newRequest) {
        request = newRequest;
    }

    public HttpServletRequest getRequest() {
        return request;
    }

    public void setResponse(HttpServletResponse newResponse) {
        response = newResponse;
    }

    public HttpServletResponse getResponse() {
        return response;
    }
```

```java
    public void setServletContext(ServletContext newContext) {
        servletContext = newContext;
    }

    public ServletContext getServletContext() {
        return servletContext;
    }
}
```

The important method in the Action class is the abstract method execute(), which all child classes must override. A sample Action subclass looks like this:

`code/neal/paramcmd/pc/ListingAction.java`

```java
public class ListingAction extends Action {

    public void execute() {
        TheModel model = getOrCreateModel();
        List sortedKeywords = getSortedKeywords(model);
        bundleAttributesForView(model, sortedKeywords);
        forwardToView();
    }

    private TheModel getOrCreateModel() {
        HttpSession session = getRequest().getSession(true);
        TheModel model = null;
        model = (TheModel) session.getAttribute("model");
        if (model == null) {
            model = new TheModel();
            session.setAttribute("model", model);
        }
        return model;
    }

    private List getSortedKeywords(TheModel model) {
        List sortedKeywords = model.getKeywords();
        Collections.sort(sortedKeywords);
        return sortedKeywords;
    }

    private void bundleAttributesForView(TheModel model,
            List sortedKeywords) {
        getRequest().setAttribute("keywords", sortedKeywords);
        getRequest().setAttribute("proposed",
                model.getProposedKeywords());
    }

    private void forwardToView() {
        forward("/Listing.jsp");
    }
}
```

To map the actions to a particular request, the framework requires some kind of document to create an association with a name (in this case, a URL parameter) and the Action class. To keep it simple, this version uses a simple Java properties file (rather than an XML configuration file), shown here:

`code/neal/paramcmd/WEB-INF/mappings.properties`

```
#Initial generation
#Thu Jan 24 17:11:27 CST 2002
formEntry=com.nealford.art.parameterizedcommands.EntryAction
listing=com.nealford.art.parameterizedcommands.ListingAction
saveAction=com.nealford.art.parameterizedcommands.SaveAction
```

The last part of the example is the controller servlet that handles invoking the requested action. The MainController appears next:

`code/neal/paramcmd/pc/MainController.java`

```java
public class MainController extends HttpServlet {
    private Properties mappings;

    public void init(ServletConfig config) throws
            ServletException {
        super.init(config);
        InputStream is = null;
        try {
            String location = config.getInitParameter("mapping");
            is = getServletContext().getResourceAsStream(location);
            mappings = new Properties();
            mappings.load(is);
        } catch (IOException iox) {
            getServletContext().log("I/O Error", iox);
            iox.printStackTrace();
        } finally {
            try {
                is.close();
            } catch (IOException ignored) {
            }
        }
    }

    public void doGet(HttpServletRequest request,
                    HttpServletResponse response) throws
                        ServletException, IOException {
❶      String command = request.getParameter("cmd");
        String actionClass = (String) mappings.get(command);
        Action action = null;
        try {
❷          action = (Action) Class.forName(actionClass).newInstance();
        } catch (ClassNotFoundException cnfx) {
            getServletContext().log("Class Not Found", cnfx);
```

```
                        cnfx.printStackTrace();
                } catch (IllegalAccessException iax) {
                    getServletContext().log("Security Exception", iax);
                } catch (InstantiationException ix) {
                    getServletContext().log("Instantiation Exception", ix);
                }
                action.setRequest(request);
                action.setResponse(response);
                action.setServletContext(getServletContext());
❸               action.execute();
        }

        public void doPost(HttpServletRequest request,
                           HttpServletResponse response) throws
                               ServletException, IOException {
            doGet(request, response);
        }
    }
```

❶ Grab the friendly name of the action from a request parameter.

❷ Instantiate the Action class using reflection.

❸ Call the execute() method inherited from Action.

If you have browsed the guts of any J2EE web framework, you'll see nothing shocking in this code. But look at it in a different light. Two types of code exist in this example: *framework* code and *configuration* code. The framework code is in the Action and MainController classes, while the configuration is in the properties file and the Action subclass, ListingAction. In this application, you are dealing with two fundamentally different types of code, with different uses. The configuration code is a DSL for configuring your web application.

Reading from Flat Files

Here's another example of a DSL lurking deep in otherwise "normal" code. The problem: we need to read billing information from a flat file excreted periodically from a mainframe. The file structure is fixed-space fields, where each service type has different fields (the first line is used to aid in counting positions):

`code/neal/strategy/input.txt`

```
#12345678901234567890123456789012345678901234567890123456789
SVCLFOWLER         10101MS0120050313.......................
SVCLHOHPE          10201DX0320050315.......................
SVCLTWO           x10301MRP220050329...........................
USGE10301TWO          x50214..7050329..............................
```

In this scenario, the first field identifies the type of service. We know that new types of services exist beyond the two declared here, and we want to insulate the application from this change. The clever way to handle this contingency is the judicious use of the Strategy design pattern. Ultimately, we want to take one of these input lines and produce a simple class like ServiceCall:

Strategy

```
code/neal/strategy/reader/ServiceCall.java
public class ServiceCall {
    public String customerName;
    public String customerId;
    public String callTypeCode;
    public String dateOfCallString;

    public String toString() {
        return "customerName: " + customerName +
                "\ncustomerId: " + customerId +
                "\ncallTypeCode " + callTypeCode +
                "\ndate of Call: " + dateOfCallString;
    }
}
```

For the first step, we configure a Reader interface that includes the interesting methods:

```
code/neal/strategy/reader/ReaderStrategy.java
public interface ReaderStrategy {
    String getCode();
    void addFieldExtractor(int begin, int end, String target);
    Object process(String line);
}
```

ReaderStrategy defines the methods that each strategy must implement: getCode() retrieves the code type, which determines what other fields to expect; the addFieldExtractor() allows us to define field positions; and process() consumes a line of our input file.

Now comes the hard part, defining the ReaderStrategyImpl that will handle defining strategies. This class utilizes an inner class to hold field information, reflection to create objects, and Java 5 generics to create type-safe collections. Hold your breath, and check out this listing (or just trust that it does what I say it does):

```
code/neal/strategy/reader/ReaderStrategyImpl.java
public class ReaderStrategyImpl implements ReaderStrategy {
    private String _code;
    private Class _target;
```

❶
```java
final class FieldExtractor {
    private int _begin, _end;
    private String _targetPropertyName;

    public FieldExtractor(int begin, int end, String target) {
        _begin = begin;
        _end = end;
        _targetPropertyName = target;
    }
```

❷
```java
    public void extractField(String line, Object targetObject) {
        String value = line.substring(_begin, _end + 1);
        try {
            setValue(targetObject, value);
        } catch (Exception oops) {
            throw new RuntimeException(oops);
        }
    }
```

❸
```java
    private void setValue(Object targetObject, String value)
        throws Exception {
        Field field = targetObject.getClass().getField(_targetPropertyName);
        field.set(targetObject, value);
    }
}
```

❹
```java
private List<ReaderStrategyImpl.FieldExtractor> extractors =
        new ArrayList<ReaderStrategyImpl.FieldExtractor>();
```

```java
public ReaderStrategyImpl(String code, Class target) {
    _code = code;
    _target = target;
}

public String getCode() {
    return _code;
}

public void addFieldExtractor(int begin, int end, String target) {
    if (! targetPropertyNames().contains(target))
        throw new NoFieldInTargetException(target, _target.getName());
    extractors.add(new ReaderStrategyImpl.FieldExtractor(begin, end, target));
}

private List<String> targetPropertyNames() {
    List<String> result = new ArrayList<String>();
    Field fields[] = _target.getFields();
    for (Field f : fields)
        result.add(f.getName());
    return result;
}
```

```
       public Object process(String line) {
           Object result = null;
           try {
               result = _target.newInstance();
           } catch (Exception oops) {
               oops.printStackTrace();
           }
❺          for (FieldExtractor ex : extractors)
               ex.extractField(line, result);
           return result;
       }
   }
```

❶ Inner class that holds an individual field extractor object

❷ Extracts the field from the fixed-width string

❸ Uses reflection to set the value of the field defined by this field
    extractor

❹ Outer class collection of field extractors that make up a single
    record from the flat file

❺ Where the action is: loops over all the field extractors and extracts
    the fields

OK, we now have all the framework set up. The last piece of the puzzle
is to use this framework to actually pull some service call records from
a sample flat file. This happens in ProcessRequest:

`code/neal/strategy/reader/ProcessRequest.java`

```
public class ProcessRequest {

    public ProcessRequest() {
        createInputFile();
        Reader reader = new Reader();
        configure(reader);
        outputResults(reader.process(getInput()));
    }

    private void outputResults(List result) {
        for (Object o : result)
            System.out.println(o);
    }

    private BufferedReader getInput() {
        BufferedReader buf = null;
        try {
            buf = new BufferedReader(new FileReader("input.txt"));
        } catch (FileNotFoundException e) {
```

```
                e.printStackTrace();
        }
        return buf;
    }

    private void configure(Reader target) {
        target.addStrategy(configureServiceCall());
        target.addStrategy(configueUsage());
    }

    private ReaderStrategy configureServiceCall() {
        ReaderStrategy result =
            new ReaderStrategyImpl("SVCL", ServiceCall.class);
        result.addFieldExtractor(4, 18, "customerName");
        result.addFieldExtractor(19, 23, "customerId");
        result.addFieldExtractor(24, 27, "callTypeCode");
        result.addFieldExtractor(28, 35, "dateOfCallString");
        return result;
    }

    private ReaderStrategy configueUsage() {
        ReaderStrategy result =
            new ReaderStrategyImpl("USGE", Usage.class);
        result.addFieldExtractor(4, 8, "customerId");
        result.addFieldExtractor(9, 22, "customerName");
        result.addFieldExtractor(23, 30, "cycle");
        result.addFieldExtractor(31, 36, "readDate");
        return result;
    }

    public static void main(String[] args) {
        new ProcessRequest();
    }
}
```

We hoped with all that framework code behind us that using the framework would be easy and, lo and behold, it is—we see very little code. Using this strategy framework means that it is easy to configure new formats for messages just by creating new methods like configureServiceCall().

Now that we've slogged through all that code, what does this have to do with domain-specific languages? Just as in the *J2EE Front Controller in Web Frameworks* section, we can partition this strategy code into *framework* and *configuration*. In this case, the framework code is the Reader infrastructure and most of ProcessRequest. The configuration code lies embedded inside ProcessRequest in two key methods: configureServiceCall() and configureUsage().

`code/neal/strategy/reader/ProcessRequest.java`

```java
private ReaderStrategy configureServiceCall() {
    ReaderStrategy result =
            new ReaderStrategyImpl("SVCL", ServiceCall.class);
    result.addFieldExtractor(4, 18, "customerName");
    result.addFieldExtractor(19, 23, "customerId");
    result.addFieldExtractor(24, 27, "callTypeCode");
    result.addFieldExtractor(28, 35, "dateOfCallString");
    return result;
}

private ReaderStrategy configueUsage() {
    ReaderStrategy result =
            new ReaderStrategyImpl("USGE", Usage.class);
    result.addFieldExtractor(4, 8, "customerId");
    result.addFieldExtractor(9, 22, "customerName");
    result.addFieldExtractor(23, 30, "cycle");
    result.addFieldExtractor(31, 36, "readDate");
    return result;
}
```

It shouldn't be a far stretch to imagine this configuration code in a separate file with a different syntax. Consider this version, in the ever-popular XML:

`code/neal/strategy/ReaderConfig.xml`

```xml
<ReaderConfiguration>
  <Mapping Code = "SVCL" TargetClass = "dsl.ServiceCall">
    <Field name = "CustomerName" start = "4" end = "18"/>
    <Field name = "CustomerID" start = "19" end = "23"/>
    <Field name = "CallTypeCode" start = "24" end = "27"/>
    <Field name = "DateOfCallString" start = "28" end = "35"/>
  </Mapping>
  <Mapping Code = "USGE" TargetClass = "dsl.Usage">
    <Field name = "CustomerID" start = "4" end = "8"/>
    <Field name = "CustomerName" start = "9" end = "22"/>
    <Field name = "Cycle" start = "30" end = "30"/>
    <Field name = "ReadDate" start = "31" end = "36"/>
  </Mapping>
</ReaderConfiguration>
```

Or, imagine it as a simple text file with the same information:

`code/neal/strategy/ReaderConfig.txt`

```
mapping SVCL dsl.ServiceCall
  4-18: CustomerName
  19-23: CustomerID
  24-27 : CallTypeCode
  28-35 : DateOfCallString
```

```
mapping  USGE dsl.Usage
  4-8 : CustomerID
  9-22: CustomerName
  30-30: Cycle
  31-36: ReadDate
```

Or, again just for fun, imaging one more syntax:

```
code/neal/strategy/ReaderConfig.rb
```
```ruby
mapping('SVCL', ServiceCall) do
        extract 4..18, 'customer_name'
        extract 19..23, 'customer_ID'
        extract 24..27, 'call_type_code'
        extract 28..35, 'date_of_call_string'
end
mapping('USGE', Usage) do
        extract 9..22, 'customer_name'
        extract 4..8, 'customer_ID'
        extract 30..30, 'cycle'
        extract 31..36, 'read_date'
end
```

As you may have guessed, that last one was Ruby code. (I couldn't write a whole chapter about DSLs without sneaking some Ruby in here somewhere, could I?)

The point is that all four representations (Java code, XML, plain text, and Ruby code) include the same information. This is the abstract

abstract syntax

concrete syntaxes

syntax of our configuration language. The four (or more) ways we can look at it are all concrete syntaxes of our language. It turns out that this distinction between abstract and concrete leads to some interesting things.

The pervasive use of XML in the Java world is really a reflection of the need to separate different languages: the language of the framework and the language of configuration. Think of all the frameworks you've used that have XML configuration files (better yet, try to think of a Java framework that *doesn't* use XML).

2.4   Building DSLs

Once you have identified a problem domain suitable for its own language, you must decide how to build it. You have two choices: internal or external. First I'll discuss your options for building an internal DSL in Java and then contrast that with building an external DSL.

Internal DSLs

An internal DSL is a new language written "on top" of the underlying   *internal DSL*
syntax of your base language (in this case, Java). Java makes it difficult
to create an English-like DSL because it has strict rules for syntax:
every statement must end with a semicolon, you must have a public
static void main(), etc.

This doesn't prevent you from creating sentence-like structures using
methods. Consider the code in the following listing, which creates an
internal DSL for a workout log:

`code/neal/exerlog/MonthlyExerLog.java`
```java
public class MonthlyExerLog {

    public static void main(String[] args) {
        new MonthlyExerLog();
    }

    public MonthlyExerLog() {
        new Log().forMonth("January").
            add(new Swim().onDate("01/02/2005").forDistance(1250)).
            add(new Bike().onDate("01/02/2005").forDistance(20)).
            add(new Swim().onDate("01/03/2005").forDistance(1500)).
            add(new Run().onDate("01/03/2005").forDistance(5)).
            report();

        Log febLog = new Log().forMonth("February");
        febLog.add(new Swim().onDate("02/01/2005").forDistance(1250));
        febLog.add(new Run().onDate("02/01/2005").forDistance(3.1));
        febLog.add(new Swim().onDate("02/24/2005").forDistance(3000));
        febLog.add(new Bike().onDate("02/25/2005").forDistance(24.5));
        febLog.report();
    }
}
```

The building blocks for this internal DSL are normal methods, written in a certain style. To allow them to chain together like English
sentences, the methods have prepositional prefixes, and all return the
instance of the object to which they are part. Consider the Exercise class:

`code/neal/exerlog/Exercise.java`
```java
abstract public class Exercise {
    private Calendar date;
    private double distance;
    private DistanceUnitOfMeasure units;

    public Calendar getDate() {
        return date;
    }
```

```java
public Exercise onDate(Calendar date) {
    this.date = date;
    return this;
}

public double getDistance() {
    return distance;
}

public Exercise forDistance(int distance) {
    this.distance = distance;
    return this;
}

public Exercise forDistance(double distance) {
    this.distance = distance;
    return this;
}

public Exercise onDate(String dateString) {
    Calendar c = Calendar.getInstance();
    String month = dateString.substring(0, dateString.indexOf('/'));
    String day = dateString.substring(dateString.indexOf("/") + 1,
            dateString.lastIndexOf("/"));
    String year = dateString.substring(dateString.lastIndexOf("/") + 1,
            dateString.length());
    c.set(Calendar.MONTH, Integer.parseInt(month) - 1);
    c.set(Calendar.DATE, Integer.parseInt(day));
    c.set(Calendar.YEAR, Integer.parseInt(year));
    date = c;
    return this;
}

public DistanceUnitOfMeasure getUnits() {
    return units;
}

public Exercise inUnits(DistanceUnitOfMeasure units) {
    this.units = units;
    return this;
}

public void add(Calendar date, int distance, DistanceUnitOfMeasure units) {

}

abstract public String getType();

public String report() {
    StringBuffer buf = new StringBuffer(100);
```

```
            buf.append("On ").
                append(new SimpleDateFormat("EEE, MMM d, yyyy").format(
                        new Date(date.getTimeInMillis()))).
                append(" ").
                append(getType()).
                append(" for distance of ").
                append(distance).
                append(" ").
                append(units.toString());
            return buf.toString();
    }
}
```

Contrast this with the "normal" Java style of writing getter() and setter() methods. The DSL style creates code that is almost as readable as English, which is, of course, the goal.

The real test, though, is whether you can give this file to an exercise physiologist to read and use. They will surely ask, "What is this main() thing?" and "Why are there so many semicolons?" Obviously, an internal DSL written in Java is for developer consumption only.

In fact, one of the best examples of this style of coding shows up in the jMock mock-object library. Here is some representative code from jMock:

```
class PublisherTest extends MockObjectTestCase {
    public void testOneSubscriberReceivesAMessage() {
        Mock mockSubscriber = mock(Subscriber.class);
        Publisher publisher = new Publisher();
        publisher.add((Subscriber) mockSubscriber.proxy());
        final String message = "message";
        // expectations
        mockSubscriber.expects(once()).method("receive").with( eq(message) );
        // execute
        publisher.publish(message);
    }
}
```

The code to set up the Mock and the Publisher looks like pretty mundane Java code. However, the configuration of mockSubscriber is very much in the DSL style. In this case, the purposely readable style indeed makes the code much more readable. Contrast this with the typical litany of setXXX() calls you would normally expect.

Internal domain-specific languages in Java really make sense only for consumption by other developers. If you don't know Java, you can never make sense of some of the required elements. To create a DSL to be used by nondevelopers, you have to switch to an external DSL.

External DSLs

An external DSL creates a new language. You need three elements to create a language: a grammar, a lexer, and a parser.

Language Building Blocks

grammar

A grammar for a computer language is just like a grammar for a spoken language (only less subjective). When creating a grammar, you lay out all the atomic elements of the language and how they fit together. These grammars may exist in a variety of formats (depending on the tool you use), but most follow BNF (the Backus-Naur Form, named for John Backus and Peter Naur) or EBNF, which is Extended Backus-Naur form (and, no, there wasn't a guy named Extended).

lexer

Once you have a grammar, you must create a lexer. A lexer is responsible for reading your input file and breaking it up into tokens, defined by your grammar. Lexers translate the actual bytes and letters into something meaningful in the context of your language.

parser

The last in the chain is the parser, which applies the grammar rules to the sequence of tokens and decides whether you have a grammatically correct statement/program and what to do in response to the code you've written in your language. You'll see an example of both a lexer and parser in the next section.

Building a Language

A variety of language construction tools exist, from the legendary and prickly LEX and YACC, to more modern (and Java-centric) tools such as ANTLR (Another Tool for Language Recognition) and the acronym-free Gold Parser System, which provides an IDE for building languages. Both ANTLR and Gold allow you to write the code that fulfills your grammar's requests in Java.

Here's a brief external DSL version of the previous exercise log example. This example uses ANTLR as the language building tool because its grammar syntax is straightforward and it allows you to embed Java code to respond to language events directly in the grammar. Ultimately, I want to create a source file that looks like this:

`code/neal/exerlang/sample.exer`

```
swim on WED for 2150
run on TUE for 6.5
bike on SAT for 50
summary
```

To create this simple language, I must first create a lexer to define all
the atomic pieces:

`code/neal/exerlang/exer.g`

```
class ExerlangLexer extends Lexer;

EXERCISE : "swim"
         | "bike"
         | "run"
         ;

WS       : (' '
         | '\t'
         | '\n'
         | '\r')
              { _ttype = Token.SKIP; }
         ;

ON       : "on";

FOR      : "for";

DISTANCE : (DIGIT)+ ;

protected
DIGIT    : '0'..'9';

WEEKDAY  : "MON"
         | "TUE"
         | "WED"
         | "THU"
         | "FRI"
         | "SAT"
         | "SUN"
         ;

SUMMARY : "summary" ;
```

Once I have defined the elements of the language, I must define how
they fit together and what to do in Java code when various parts of my
language appear. This happens in the parser (which, in ANTLR, may
appear in the same file as the lexer).

`code/neal/exerlang/exer.g`

```
class ExerlangParser extends Parser;

options {
    buildAST = true;
}
```

```
series
    : EXERCISE ON! WEEKDAY FOR! DISTANCE
    | SUMMARY
    ;

class ExerLangTreeParser extends TreeParser;
{
    int swim = 0;
    int bike = 0;
    int run = 0;
}

sum
    : e:EXERCISE

        d:WEEKDAY {
            System.out.print("on " + d.getText());
        }

        dist:DISTANCE {
            System.out.println(" went " + dist.getText());
            if (e.getText().equals("swim"))
                swim += Integer.parseInt(dist.getText());
             else if (e.getText().equals("bike"))
                bike += Integer.parseInt(dist.getText());
            else
                run += Integer.parseInt(dist.getText());
        }
    ;

total
    : SUMMARY {
            System.out.println("Summary: \n-----------");
            System.out.println("Swim:  " + swim);
            System.out.println("Bike:  " + bike);
            System.out.println("Run:" + run);
        }
    ;
```

As you can see, ANTLR allows you to place variables and Java code
directly in the grammar. In this case, I put all the behavior of the language inline in the grammar. For more complex projects, you typically
create a class to hold that state and execute one-line method calls from
the grammar to your state class.

Once the lexer and parser are completed, you can run the ANTLR tool
on it to generate the lexer and parser Java source files. These source
files are simultaneously ugly, complex, and never in need of hand editing. What these files allow, though, is the creation of a simple Java
class with a main() method to apply your language to a source file:

`code/neal/exerlang/Main.java`

```java
public class Main {

    public static void main(String[] args) {
        Reader reader = null;
        try {
            reader = new FileReader(args[0]);
        } catch (FileNotFoundException e) {
            e.printStackTrace();
        }
        // attach lexer to the input stream
        ExerlangLexer lexer = new ExerlangLexer(reader);

        // Create parser attached to lexer
        ExerlangParser parser = new ExerlangParser(lexer);

        // start up the parser by calling the rule
        // at which you want to begin parsing.

        try {
            parser.series();


            // Get the tree out of the parser
            AST resultTree = parser.getAST();

            // Make an instance of the tree parser
            ExerLangTreeParser treeParser = new ExerLangTreeParser();

            treeParser.sum(resultTree);  // walk AST once
        } catch (RecognitionException e) {
            e.printStackTrace();
        } catch (TokenStreamException e) {
            e.printStackTrace();
        }
    }
}
```

Whew! A five-page introduction to compiler theory and building a new language. It seems pretty complex, doesn't it? Well, it is. And this complexity is one of the reasons this style of programming hasn't really achieved its potential. What we need are tools to make this process much easier. They are on the way....

2.5 Language Workbenches

Programming by writing DSLs has moved beyond academia and the small pools of developers who have used it to gain advantages in limited

language workbenches

problem domains. At least three major software vendors are actively pursuing the idea of language-oriented programming by building language workbenches:

- JetBrains MPS (Meta-Programming System)

- Microsoft, with its Software Factories and a Visual Studio DSL plug-in

- Intentional Software, producing something it will not talk about publicly

All these tools (with the possible exception of Intentional's, because no one knows) are in the early stages of development. But the industry interest in this style of building software is noteworthy. Language workbenches make building external DSLs much easier by providing specialized editors, code generation, prebuilt classes, and other tools.

symbolic integration

As an example of the support these tools afford, consider the problem of symbolic integration. If you create an external DSL now, you must edit it in a text editor. At best, you can create a syntax file for some existing editors, but you don't get that to which you are accustomed: context-sensitive pull-down syntax help, refactoring, debugging, and all the other accoutrements we have for traditional languages. This is the symbolic integration of our editors to our languages.

MPS, from JetBrains, changes that. When you design a language, you also design an editor that provides context-sensitive pull-down lists, syntax highlighting, and the other types of symbolic integration we all crave. For example, Figure 2.1, on the facing page shows an editor for a DSL concerning the problem domain of billing rates and dates. MPS allows the developer to create the DSL, symbolically integrated editor, and code generator for any language you can conceive.

2.6 Summary

Internal DSLs are easier to write because you leverage existing tools and language elements. Whether these DSL are usable by people who aren't programmers depends largely on the flexibility (and forgiveness) of the language.

External DSLs allow you to create any type of language you want, governed only by your ability to parse the code and apply rules to it. Currently, these languages present great hurdles because of the primitive

```
plan LowPay

    value Quantity BASE RATE
          1999 - 10 - 01 :   10.0 USD/KwH
    value Quantity REDUCED RATE
          1999 - 10 - 01 :   5.0 USD/KwH
          yyyy - mm - dd :   2.2 USD/KwH
    value Quantity CAP
          1999 - 10 - 01 :   50.0 KwH

    event USAGE
          1999 - 10 - 01 :   amount  : IF( usage > CAP , BASE RATE * usage , REDUCED RATE * usage )
                             account : base-usage
    event SERVICE CALL
          1999 - 10 - 01 :   amount  : $ 10.0 +
                             account : service   +            jetbrains.mps.formulaLanguage.structure
          1999 - 12 - 01 :   amount  : fee * 0.5 -            jetbrains.mps.formulaLanguage.structure
                             account : service   <            jetbrains.mps.formulaLanguage.structure
    event TAX                                    >            jetbrains.mps.formulaLanguage.structure
          1999 - 10 - 01 :   amount  : fee * 0.0 BASE RATE
                             account : tax        CAP
                                                  IF(,,)      jetbrains.mps.formulaLanguage.structure
                                                  REDUCED RATE
                                                  fee

                                                  quantity
                                                  integer constant (formula language)
```

Figure 2.1: MPS EDITOR FOR A DSL

nature of the tools we must use to build them. Help is on the horizon as language workbenches appear.

This style of programming has the potential to be the next evolutionary step beyond object-oriented programming. One of the strengths of OOP is its ability to encapsulate messy details into hierarchies. But it turns out that the entire world cannot be shoehorned into a tree shape, which is why we have features such as aspects to cut across the trees.

OOP has served us well, but it is too low a level of abstraction. We need to use objects, aspects, and other building blocks to upgrade our abstraction and build languages closer to the problem domains where we work. The Lisp and Smalltalk guys who built DSLs were right: the closer you can model your problem domain, the more productive you are because you work right on top of the problem. Although classes are fine, we need a higher layer of abstraction—*languages* close to the problem domain. Language-oriented programming will be the next major paradigm shift in the way we build software. And it's about time!

Chapter 3

Shale

by David Geary

A prominent author, speaker, and consultant, David Geary holds a unique qualification as a Java expert: He wrote the best-selling books on each of Java's component frameworks: Swing and JavaServer Faces (JSF). David's Graphic Java Swing [Gea99] was one of the best-selling Java books of all time, and Core JavaServer Faces [GH04], which he wrote with Cay Horstmann, is the most popular JSF book.

David was one of a handful of experts on the JSF Expert Group that actively defined the standard Java-based web application framework. Besides serving on the JSF and JSTL Expert Groups, David has contributed to open source projects and coauthored Sun's Web Developer Certification Exam. He invented the Struts Template library that was the precursor to Tiles, a popular framework for composing web pages from JSP fragments, was the second Struts committer and is currently an active contributor to Shale.

A regular on the NFJS tour, David also speaks at other conferences such as JavaOne and JavaPolis. In 2005, David was awarded a Top Speaker award at JavaOne for his Shale presentation with Craig McClanahan.

At NFJS, David loves to interact with attendees and is known for his sense of humor, dazzling demos, and electrifying live-coding sessions.

Released in the spring of 2004 after nearly three years in the making, JavaServer Faces (JSF) was met with a healthy dose of skepticism. You can hardly blame Java developers for being skeptical. After all, many had suffered irreparable damage from their encounters with EJB. Another official spec from Sun for the other side of the house? Not for us, thanks.

But JSF is an excellent framework, as most people realize once they use it. Witness Gavin King, who chose JSF as his UI framework for his Ruby on Rails killer, Seam:

"I was casting around for a framework to marry with EJB3.... I was expecting [JSF] to be a bit of a steaming pile.... Rather, I found that once I sat down and looked at it...it was basically how I would think to define a framework."[1]

3.1 The Frameworks

Gavin King is not alone in his opinion of JSF. In fact, Gavin's framework, Seam, is just one of the impressive frameworks based on JSF that have emerged in the very recent past:

- Shale
- Facelets
- MyFaces
- Tomahawk
- JBoss's Seam
- Oracle's ADF

All the preceding projects are open source, and nobody gives up their social life to start an open source project based on a framework they perceive as a failure. As Eminem says, "I ain't had to graduate from Lincoln High School to know that." The sudden emergence of high-quality, sophisticated frameworks built on top of JSF, such as Shale, Facelets, MyFaces components, and JBoss's Seam are a clear signal to the industry that JSF is for real.

Of course, you may ask yourself, "If JSF is such a great framework, then why does it need all those other frameworks?" Good question. The truth is that the current version of JSF has numerous holes. For example, out of the box, JSF does not explicitly support client-side

---

[1]From the Java Posse's interview with Gavin

validation. JSF also uses JSP as its default display technology; if you're not happy with that choice, you could bolt on your own view technology, but are you really going to do that? Probably not.

Open source to the rescue! MyFaces gives you a solid alternative to the JSF Reference Implementation and a nice set of components to boot. Facelets gives you Tapestry-like views and support for page composition that rivals its more sophisticated cousin, Tiles. Seam, inspired by Ruby on Rails, unifies the EJB 3.0 and JSF component models in a radical recasting of the JEE landscape. And then there's Shale, which is the object of our immediate interest.

3.2 Enter Shale

The inventor of the most popular Java-based web application framework is strongly in favor of abandoning the current code base in favor of an entirely new framework built on JSF. In 2005, Craig McClanahan proposed his nascent Shale framework, built on JSF, as a successor to Struts.

Shale, which is a set of services built on top of JSF, has nothing to do with the original Struts. In fact, the original Struts has forked into two branches: Shale and Action. Shale hitches a ride on JSF, whereas Action is a merger of Struts Classic and WebWork.

Since its inception in 2005, other Struts committers have jumped on the Shale bandwagon, including the author of this article, and Shale has matured into a robust set of services built on JSF:

- Tapestry-like views
- Web flow
- Method remoting (basis for Ajax)
- Support for JDK 5.0 annotations
- Apache Commons validator integration
- Testing framework, integrated with HTMLUnit
- Integration with Spring, Tiles, and JNDI
- View controllers

What does all that mean? It means you can strictly separate the roles of graphic designer and software developer with Shale's powerful Clay plug-in that provides other goodies such as parameterizing chunks of JSP with symbols so JSP can be reused for different managed beans. It means you can define the flow of a user conversation—a set of HTTP requests between the user and the application—in an XML file, sort of a souped-up version of JSF's default navigation. It means you can easily call any managed bean method from JavaScript, which gives you the foundation for Ajax. And that's just the beginning.

3.3 Common Use Cases

In 2005, Shale grew from a handful of utilities to a robust set of services built on JSF. A comprehensive examination of Shale would require a book of its own, so here I will concentrate on three of the more interesting use cases that Shale supports:

- Ajax
- Web flow
- HTML views

Ajax

I was on a plane on the way home from the 2006 St. Louis show when the guy sitting next to me asked me what I did for a living. I told him about NFJS, and it just so happened that I was working on my Ajaxian Faces presentation at that very moment, so I showed him a progress bar that I'd developed for that talk. "This is really cutting-edge stuff," I told the guy. "We haven't been able to effectively refresh parts of a page like that before. People at the show will be excited about this." I turned to look at the guy and he had cocked his head and raised one eyebrow as if to say, "You're joking, right?" At that moment, it occurred to me how lucky software developers are compared to, say, astrophysicists, who don't stand a snowball's chance in hell of explaining what they do to the common man.

So, in deference to humble accomplishments, I present an example that uses Shale method remoting to perform real-time validation. When the user exits the username text field, we'll sneak a quick trip to the server and, via some Ajaxian magic, return a response, either positive or negative, for the username the user left behind in the text field.

As you can see from Figure 3.1, on the next page, the only username taken is Joe, so we react accordingly when confronted with either Joe or anything but Joe. Let's look at some code. First, here's the view:

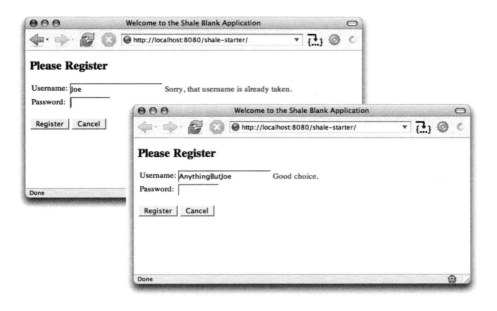

Figure 3.1: REAL-TIME VALIDATION FAILS THEN SUCCEEDS

```
<h:form>
  <h:panelGrid columns="2">
    <h:outputText value="Username:"/>
    <h:panelGroup>
      <h:inputText onfocus="hideMessage();"
                   onblur="validateUsername(this.value);"/>
      <f:verbatim>
        <div id="message" style="display: none;"></div>
      </f:verbatim>
    </h:panelGroup>

    <h:outputText value="Password:"/>
    <h:inputText size="8"/>
  </h:panelGrid>
</h:form>
```

The code reacts to onfocus and onblur events. The validateUsername()
JavaScript function, to which we pass the current value of the text
field, sends an Ajax request to Shale, which in turn invokes a method
on a managed bean. That method returns some XML, which we subsequently use to update the hidden *<div>* with the id of message. You've
no doubt seen this sort of trickery before. Here's the corresponding
JavaScript:

```
<script src="prototype.js"></script> <!-- Prototype JavaScript Library -->

<script type="text/javascript" language="Javascript1.1">
  <!--
  function validateUsername(username) {
      var ajaxRequest = new Ajax.Updater(
              "message",
              "dynamic/welcome/validateUsername.faces",
              {      method: "get",
                 parameters: "username=" + username,
                 onComplete: showMessage
              });
  }

  function showMessage(xhr) {
      var msg = $("message");
      msg.style.display = "inline";
      msg.style.color = "red";
  }

  function hideMessage() {
      $("message").style.display = "none";
  }
  -->
</script>
```

Implementing Ajax without a JavaScript framework is a little like using JSPs without a framework. You can do it, but why suffer? In this example, I'm using the Prototype JavaScript library, which, ironically enough, is the foundation upon which Ruby on Rails' Ajax is implemented. But that's another NFJS session.

Notice the URL we pass in to Prototype's Ajax.Updater() constructor: dynamic/welcome/validateUsername.faces. The instance of Ajax.Updater() that we create uses the mythical XMLHttpRequest object to invoke that URL on the server. Here's the catch: that URL means something to Shale; specifically, a URL that begins with dynamic is taken to be a remote method call. When Shale sees that our URL starts with dynamic, it invokes this method: welcome.validateUsername(), where welcome is a managed bean defined in your application and validateUsername() is a method of that bean. That means you can invoke a server-side method from JavaScript code anytime, with no fuss. That's Shale remoting. All that's left is the rather mundane bean code:

```
public void validateUsername() {
  String username = (String)getRequestParameterMap().get("username");
  if("Joe".equals(username))
    writeResponse("Sorry, that username is already taken.");
```

```
    else
      writeResponse("Good choice.");
  }
  private void writeResponse(String text) {
    FacesContext context = getFacesContext();
    ResponseWriter writer =
      (new ResponseFactory()).getResponseWriter(context, "text/xml");
    try {
      writer.startDocument();
      writer.startElement("value", null);
      writer.writeText(text, null);
      writer.endElement("value");
      writer.endDocument();
    }
    catch (IOException e) {
      e.printStackTrace();
    }
    context.responseComplete();
  }
}
```

Notice the mysterious ResponseFactory. That's a Shale remoting object that simplifies writing a response; in this case, it's our XML response. Before the writeResponse() method returns, it calls responseComplete() on the Faces context, which short-circuits the JSF life cycle. JSF does not render a response; instead, it assumes we've written to the response ourselves, which of course we have.

Web Flow

JSF provides navigation facilities that are capable enough for most applications, but JSF doesn't explicitly support higher-level constructs such as wizards. Shale provides support for more creative navigation with its Web Flow package, which is modeled after Spring Web Flow with a decidedly JSF perspective. Defining a web flow is simple to do.

Figure 3.2, on the following page and Figure 3.3, on the next page show two screens from a wizard. You can see links to the five wizard panels in the sidebar on the left side of the window. The current panel's link is italic, so it's readily apparent what panel the user is on. The wizard buttons are also sensitive to the currently displayed panel. All of that sensitivity is implemented by obtaining the current state of the dialog from Shale and then deciding on the state of user interface elements; for example, on the Username and Password panel there is no previous panel, so the Previous button is disabled, but on the Phone Numbers panel, there is a previous panel (Username and Password), so the Previous button is enabled for the Phone Numbers panel.

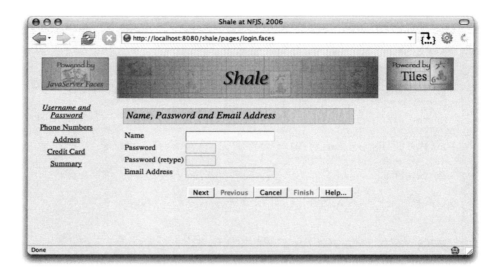

Figure 3.2: THE USERNAME WIZARD PANEL

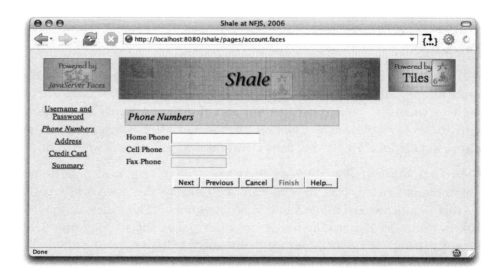

Figure 3.3: THE PHONE NUMBERS WIZARD PANEL

Here's the Shale XML definition for the wizard:

```
<dialogs>
  <dialog          name="Create Account"  start="User Information">

    <!-- Transitions applicable to all states -->
    <transition  outcome="cancel"        target="Exit"/>
    <transition  outcome="username"      target="User Information"/>
    <transition  outcome="phoneNumbers"  target="Phone Numbers"/>
    <transition  outcome="address"       target="Address"/>
    <transition  outcome="creditCard"    target="Credit Card"/>
    <transition  outcome="summary"       target="Summary"/>

    <!-- User Information -->
    <view        name="User Information"
                 viewId="/pages/account.jsp">
      <transition outcome="next"
                 target="Phone Numbers"/>
    </view>

    <!-- Phone Numbers -->
    <view        name="Phone Numbers"
                 viewId="/pages/account.jsp">
      <transition outcome="next"
                 target="Address"/>
      <transition outcome="previous"
                 target="User Information"/>
    </view>

    <!-- Address -->
    <view        name="Address"
                 viewId="/pages/account.jsp">
      <transition outcome="next"
                 target="Credit Card"/>
      <transition outcome="previous"
                 target="Phone Numbers"/>
    </view>

    ...
    <!-- Credit Card -->
    <view        name="Credit Card"
                 viewId="/pages/account.jsp">
      <transition outcome="next"
                 target="Summary"/>
      <transition outcome="previous"
                 target="Address"/>
      <transition outcome="finish"
                 target="Create User"/>
    </view>
```

```
<!-- Summary -->
<view         name="Summary"
              viewId="/pages/account.jsp">
  <transition outcome="previous"
              target="Credit Card"/>
  <transition outcome="finish"
              target="Create User"/>
</view>

<!-- Create User -->
<action       name="Create User"
              method="#{accountPage.finish}">
  <transition outcome="finish"
              target="Exit"/>
</action>

<!-- Exit -->
<end          name="Exit" viewId="/pages/login.jsp"/>
  </dialog>
</dialogs>
```

It's pretty easy to understand the preceding XML, even if you know nothing about Shale. Each of the five panels is represented with a view element. Views, or *view states*, as they are known, can have transitions that take you to the next state. For example, when Shale loads the Create Account dialog, it starts with the User Information state, which loads pages/account.jsp/. Then Shale waits for the user to click a link or activate a button, and it looks at the corresponding outcome. If the outcome matches a transition element, Shale forwards to that state and waits for the next outcome, which triggers the next transition. A special state, specified by the end element, cleans up any state that Shale has stored, including a status object full of information about the current dialog that you can programmatically access.

Method remoting and web flow are two of Shale's hallmark features. Before we wrap up, I'd like to show you one other really cool feature: Clay.

HTML Views

Back in the old days, through the magic of servlets, everybody emitted HTML from Java print statements. Imagine. Nowadays, especially in the JSF world, we pretty much stick to JSP and custom tags, which encapsulate a great deal of noise and let us work at a higher level of abstraction. That's great for developers who are also graphic designers,

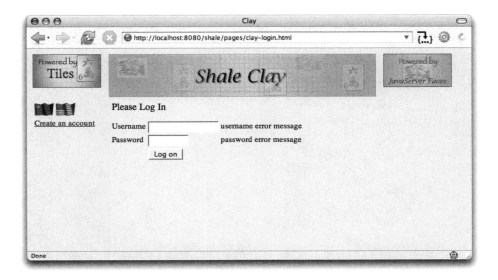

Figure 3.4: HTML MOCK-UP WITH CLAY

but if you've ever had to merge a designer's HTML mock-up's look and feel into a nontrivial JSF application replete with deeply nested Tiles, you've experienced the dark side of custom tags firsthand.

Sometimes, as Tapestry advocates will argue (and rightly so), it's best to separate the responsibilities of graphic design and software development so that each can implement their code without dependencies upon the other. Like Tapestry, Shale's Clay supports HTML views, where the only perceptible variation from vanilla HTML is the presence of a jsfid= attribute.

With Clay, user interfaces are defined in HTML (which does not have to be well-formed, by the way). Typically, software developers create some simple HTML mock-up and hand the HTML to the designer, who subsequently adds a look and feel and returns the HTML to the developer. That single HTML file serves two purposes. When viewed directly in a browser or another HTML-viewing tool such as Dreamweaver, you see the mock-up HTML and its corresponding look and feel. But when that same HTML file is run through Shale's Clay, *the mock-up HTML is replaced with JSF components that have absorbed the mock-up's look and feel.* For example, take a look at Figure 3.4.

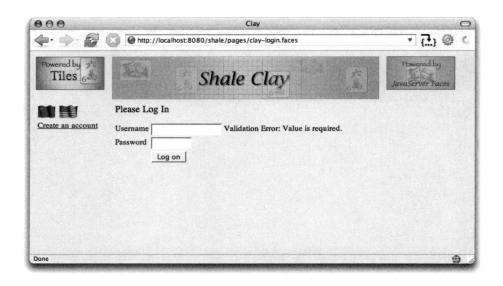

Figure 3.5: JSF COMPONENTS REPLACE MOCK-UP HTML

Figure 3.4 shows the HTML page when viewed directly (note the address bar). Figure 3.5 shows the HTML page when accessed through Shale (again, note the address bar). In Figure 3.4, we see markup for error messages, whereas in Figure 3.5 we see a message generated by the server in response to a validation failure.

How can one HTML page serve two purposes? The answer lies in the HTML itself:

```
<span jsfid="usernameMessage">
  username error message
</span>
```

Notice the jsfid= attribute. That attribute points to a JSF component that Shale's Clay substitutes for the HTML markup. What does an HTML viewer think of the jsfid= attribute? Nothing! It just ignores it and shows the markup. But when Clay parses the page and produces a view, it links in a JSF component, which is defined in a separate HTML file:

```
<component jsfid="usernameMessage" extends="message" allowBody="false">
  <attributes>
    <set name="for" value="username" />
  </attributes>
</component>
```

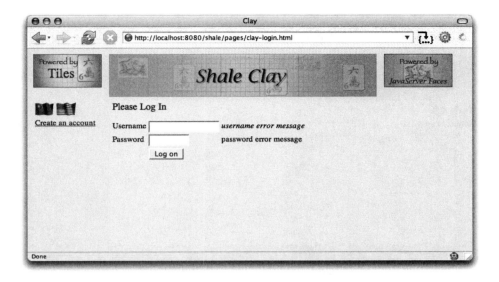

Figure 3.6: MODIFICATIONS TO HTML MOCK-UP

Now, suppose you're the graphic designer and you decide to make errors italic. So, you modify the mock-up HTML, taking great care, of course, not to disturb the jsfid attribute:

```
<span style="font-style: italic;" jsfid="usernameMessage">
  username error message
</span>
```

Now, when you look at the HTML page directly in the browser, you obtain instant gratification, as shown in Figure 3.6.

But what about the message component that replaces the mock-up HTML at runtime? Does that component absorb the look and feel of its corresponding mock-up? Of course! See Figure 3.7, on the next page.

HTML views, interestingly enough, were an afterthought to Clay, which started out as a sort of templating engine for JSF. Because of that history, Clay contains a number of other useful features such as aliasing a JSP fragment so that the fragment can be used with different managed beans.

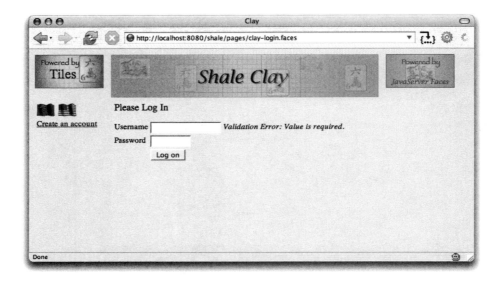

Figure 3.7: JSF COMPONENTS ABSORB HTML MOCK-UP STYLES

3.4 Wrap-up

Shale is a powerful set of services built on top of a powerful framework. As powerful as JSF is, however, the Shale developers are intimately familiar with its drawbacks and are working to overcome them to make JSF an even more appealing framework for enterprise developers.

Chapter 4

Test Categorization Techniques

by Andrew Glover

Andrew Glover is the president of Stelligent Incorporated. Stelligent helps companies address software quality with effective developer testing strategies and continuous integration techniques that enable teams to monitor code quality early and often.

Andrew was the founder of Vanward Technologies, which was acquired by JNet-Direct in 2005. He coauthored Java Testing Patterns [TYBG04] and is an author for multiple online publications including IBM's developerWorks and Oreilly's ONJava and ONLamp portals. He actively blogs about software quality at http://www.thediscoblog.com.

His thoughts on books and tools start on page 217.

Ever run a build that lasted four hours? Probably once, right? After that, you figured out how to compile just your own stuff so you could actually get some work done and not have to wait around for the entire build saga to end.

Then the rest of the team figured out how to do the same thing. Unfortunately, a day before the big release (and before you installed a continuous integration system), someone actually ran the complete build and, lo and behold, tests started failing (two hours into the build, however).

continuous integration

Unless a build compiles millions (and millions) of files, the culprit of a prolonged build is usually the testing step, which could be a series of steps! The total time to run a series of tests has the additional tendency to become longer when there are extensive setup steps too, such as configuring a database or deploying a .war file, to name a few.

For any nontrivial software project that wants to keep build times bearable, it becomes paramount to create an effective strategy for the categorization of tests. By segregating tests into categories and running the associated categories at prescribed intervals, build times can remain manageable for developers and continuous integration systems alike.

categorization of tests

We as developers tend to use the term *unit test* rather broadly. This can cause confusion, especially when teams start claiming their unit tests "take too long to run." Defining a common vocabulary for developer tests can assist in categorizing them into groups, which will make all the difference in creating an effective build process.

4.1 Unit Tests

Unit tests verify the behavior of small elements in a software system, which are most often single classes. Occasionally, though, the one-to-one relationship between a unit test and a class is slightly augmented with additional classes because the classes being tested are tightly coupled. Because of this small issue, it can be helpful to further segregate unit tests into two types: isolated and semi-isolated unit tests.

isolated

semi-isolated

TestNG

For example, the following TestNG test demonstrates an isolated unit test focussing on one object (PartOfSpeechEnum).

```
//imports removed...
/**
 * @testng.test groups="unit"
 */
public class PartOfSpeechEnumTestNG {

 public void verifyNotEquals() throws Exception{
  assert PartOfSpeechEnum.ADJECTIVE != PartOfSpeechEnum.NOUN: "Noun == Adjective!";
 }

 public void verifyEquals() throws Exception{
  assert PartOfSpeechEnum.VERB == PartOfSpeechEnum.VERB: "Verb != Verb!";
 }
}
```

Semi-isolated unit tests verify the behavior of more than one object; however, these objects have few other outside dependencies. For example, the following test verifies two objects (Dependency and Dependency-Finder):

```
//imports removed...
public class DependencyFinderTest extends TestCase {
 private DependencyFinder finder;

 public void testFindDependencies() throws Exception{
  String targetClss = "test.com.vanward.sedona.DependencyFinderTest";

  Filter[] filtr =
    new Filter[] {new RegexPackageFilter("java|junit|org|com.jcoverage")};

  Dependency[] deps = finder.findDependencies(targetClss, filtr);

  assertNotNull("deps was null", deps);
  assertEquals("should be 5 large", 5, deps.length);
 }

 protected void setUp() throws Exception {
  this.finder = new DependencyFinder();
 }
}
```

The key aspect, however, is that unit tests (regardless of isolation) do not rely on outside dependencies such as databases, which have the tendency to increase the amount of time it takes to set up and run tests.

Unit tests can be created and run early in the development cycle (day one is a good place to start). And, because of the short amount of time between coding and testing the results, unit tests are an extremely efficient way of debugging.

Because unit tests run so quickly, they should be run anytime a build is run. The whole mantra of "code a little, test a little, code a little" is predicated on the notion of rapid testing. If unit testing takes enough time that someone can focus on something else, it's taking too long! It will become a burden and, soon forgotten.

In a continuous integration, or CI, environment, builds are run anytime someone changes a source repository; therefore, unit tests should be run anytime someone checks in code. There is no configuration cost, and the resource consumption cost to run them is negligible.

4.2 Component Tests

Component or subsystem tests verify portions of a system and may require a fully installed system or a more limited set of external dependencies, such as databases, file systems, or network endpoints, to name a few. These tests verify that components interact to produce the expected aggregate behavior.

A typical component test requires the underlying database to be running and may even cross architectural boundaries. Because larger amounts of code are exercised by each test case, more code coverage is obtained per test; however, these tests have the tendency to take longer to run than unit tests.

integration test

One key difference between component-level tests and higher-level testing, like system tests (defined next), is that component-level tests exercise code via an API, which may or may not be exposed to clients. This type of test is also commonly referred to as an integration test.

Component tests should be run at regular intervals, but not necessarily every time a build is run. These tests have a cost to them—dependencies have to be put in place and configured. Moreover, these tests alone may take only a few seconds; however, in the aggregate, this time adds up.

For example, the following component test takes, on average, four seconds to run:

```java
//imports removed..

public class DefaultSpringWordDAOImplTest extends DatabaseTestCase {
 private WordDAO dao = null;

 protected IDatabaseConnection getConnection() throws Exception {
  final Class driverClass = Class.forName("org.gjt.mm.mysql.Driver");
  return new DatabaseConnection(
    DriverManager.getConnection("jdbc:mysql://localhost/words",
      "words", "words"));
 }

 protected IDataSet getDataSet() throws Exception {
  return new FlatXmlDataSet(new File("test/conf/words-seed.xml"));
 }

 public void testCreate() throws Exception{
  final IWord word = new Word();
  word.setSpelling("wamble");
  word.setPartOfSpeech(PartOfSpeechEnum.VERB.getPartOfSpeech());

  final Set definitions = this.getDefinitionForWord(word);
  word.setDefinitions(definitions);

  try{
   this.dao.createWord(word);
  } catch(CreateException e){
   TestCase.fail("CreateException thrown while trying to create a word");
  }
 }

 private Set getDefinitionForWord(IWord word){
  final IDefinition defOne = new Definition();
  defOne.setDefinition("To move unsteadily; to totter, waver, roll, etc.");
  defOne.setWord(word);

  Set defs = new HashSet();
  defs.add(defOne);
  return defs;
 }

 protected void setUp() throws Exception {
  super.setUp();
  final ApplicationContext context =
  new ClassPathXmlApplicationContext("spring-config.xml");
  this.dao = (WordDAO) context.getBean("wordDAO");
 }
}
```

DbUnit

This test does a number of things that add to the total test time and configuration complexity. First, this test seeds a database via DbUnit. In this case, DbUnit does an insert of the data found in the XML file words-seed.xml, which also implies that XML parsing is being done. This also assumes the test case can find the file easily.

Spring

Hibernate

Next, this test case configures Spring, which also configures Hibernate. Finally, a test is run and a word is retrieved from the database. Are you surprised this takes four seconds? Keep in mind, this is only one test case. Each additional test case in this class may not add another four seconds; however, it'll probably add about two seconds. Do this about ten more times and you have a minute. Get the picture?

Although these types of tests shouldn't be executed every time a build is run, it's a good bet to run them before committing code into a repository. In a CI environment, it's probably a good idea to run these at least a few times a day. Running them every time someone checks in code could cause issues; however, this takes good judgment. Some projects can get away with running component-level tests in a CI environment every time someone checks in code.

4.3 System Tests

System tests exercise a complete software system and therefore require a fully installed system, such as a servlet container and associated database. These tests verify that external interfaces, such as web pages, web service endpoints, or GUIs, work end-to-end as designed.

Because these tests exercise an entire system, they are often created in the later cycles of development. Often, these tests tend to have lengthy run times, in addition to long setup times. For example, the following

JWebUnit

test utilizes JWebUnit to test the login functionality of a website:

```
//imports removed...
public class LoginTest extends WebTestCase {
 protected void setUp() throws Exception {
   getTestContext().setBaseUrl("http://divine.google.com/con/");
 }

 public void testLogIn() {
  beginAt("/");
  setFormElement("j_username", "ajudig");
  setFormElement("j_password", "jslie");
  submit();
  assertTextPresent("Logged in as julie");
 }
}
```

Keep in mind that these tests are fundamentally different from functional tests, which test a system much like a client would use the system.

System tests, which require a fully installed system, take the longest to run. Additionally, the complexity in configuring a fully functional system occasionally prohibits the full automation of these tests.

Ideally, developers can run these tests locally when needed. In a CI environment, nightly (if they can be pulled off in an automated fashion) is a good bet with these tests. Running these tests frequently in a CI environment could be a recipe for disaster and probably overkill if other tests are run often. Sometimes at the end of release cycles, though, these types of tests can be run on a more frequent interval.

4.4 Implementing Test Categories

Frameworks such as JUnit and TestNG have annotations, which make categorizing tests quite easy to implement. However, in other frameworks, segregating tests is a bit more challenging. *JUnit*

Pre-4.0 JUnit Categorization

With pre-4.0 JUnit versions, there is no mechanism within the framework itself or within Ant to easily divide tests into three groups. This can be achieved, however, with a simple *naming scheme* or, even easier, with a *directory strategy*.

A best practice for developer testing is to place unit tests in a different directory than the source code. For example, a project would have a src folder for the source code and a test folder for associated tests:

```
$ ls -lt ./
total 62
drwx------+ 6   Andy.Glover usrs       0 Feb 19 21:37 test
drwx------+ 4   Andy.Glover usrs       0 Dec 27 21:20 src
-rwx------+ 1   Andy.Glover usrs   32452 Nov 15 17:51 build.xml
-rwx------+ 1   Andy.Glover usrs     260 Aug 30  2005 build.properties
```

The src directory would obviously contain directories which map to source code packages. With the test directory, categorization is possible by creating three additional internal directories: unit, component, and system.

For example, the directory listing would look like this:

```
$ ls -ltr ./test
total 0
drwx------+ 4 Andy.Glover usrs    0 Mar  1 22:09 unit
drwx------+ 2 Andy.Glover usrs    0 Mar  1 22:09 conf
drwx------+ 4 Andy.Glover usrs    0 Mar  1 22:11 component
drwx------+ 3 Andy.Glover usrs    0 Mar  1 22:12 system
```

The unit, component, and system directories would then contain the associated tests for each category. Note, the conf directory would hold associated properties files, and so on, required for testing.

The unit directory, for example, would have a directory structure that maps to the unit tests' package names, which usually map to the corresponding packages in the class under test, like this:

```
$ ls -ltr ./test/unit/test/com/van/sedna/frmwrk/filter/
total 12
-rwx------+ 1 Andy.Glover usrs 1190 Oct 25  2004  SimFilterTest.java
-rwx------+ 1 Andy.Glover usrs 2708 Oct 25  2004  RegexFilterTest.java
-rwx------+ 1 Andy.Glover usrs 1678 Nov 20 17:30  ClassFilterTest.java
```

Ant

Now that the tests are segregated into separate directories, your chosen build system needs an update. In the case of Ant, three targets are created. One, for running unit tests, another, for running component tests, and another, for running those system tests. A fourth target could also be created that calls all three of the previous targets so as to run the entire test suite.

For example, for system tests, the all too familiar batchtest element of the JUnit task would look something like this:

```
<batchtest todir="${testreportdir}">
  <fileset dir="test/system">
    <include name="**/*Test.*">
    </include>
  </fileset>
</batchtest>
```

Note how there isn't any special naming scheme going on here—tests are still appended with Test regardless of granularity.

If the target for running the system tests were named test-system, then running it would be as simple as typing anttest-system (don't forget to set up the associated depends clause for compiling, deploying, etc.).

TestNG Categorization

Categorizing TestNG tests into three groups (unit, component, and system) is as easy as using the group annotation (or javadoc tag with pre-

Java 5 versions). With this annotation, you can tag an entire class or an individual test method as belonging to a group.

For example, the following class has been tagged as belonging to the unit test group:

```
//imports removed
/**
 * @testng.test groups="unit"
 */
public class SimplePackageFilterTest {
/**
 * @testng.test
 */
 public void testJavaPackage() throws Exception{
  Filter fltr = new SimplePackageFilter("java.");
  String pck = "java.lang.String";
  boolean val = fltr.applyFilter(pck);
  Assert.assertTrue(val, "value should be true");
 }
/**
 * @testng.test
 */
 public void testJavaStarPackage() throws Exception{
  Filter fltr = new SimplePackageFilter("java.*");
  String pck = "java.lang.String";
  boolean val = fltr.applyFilter(pck);
  Assert.assertFalse(val, "value should be flase");
 }
}
```

Similarly, defining a test in the component group requires defining the proper group:

```
//imports removed
/**
 * @testng.test groups="component"
 */
public class BatchDepXMLReportValidationTest {
 /**
  * @testng.test
  */
 public void assertToXML() throws Exception{
  BatchDependencyXMLReport report =
    new BatchDependencyXMLReport(new Date(9000000),
         this.getFilters());

  report.addTargetAndDependencies("com.vanward.test.MyTest",
     this.getDependencies());
  report.addTargetAndDependencies("com.xom.xml.Test",
     this.getDependencies());
```

```java
  Diff diff = new Diff(new FileReader(
    new File("./test/conf/report-control.xml")),
    new StringReader(report.toXML())));
  Assert.assertTrue(diff.identical(),"XML was not identical");
}
/**
 * @testng.configuration beforeTestClass = "true" groups="component"
 */
protected void configure() throws Exception {
 XMLUnit.setControlParser("org.apache.xerces.jaxp.DocumentBuilderFactoryImpl");
 XMLUnit.setTestParser("org.apache.xerces.jaxp.DocumentBuilderFactoryImpl");
 XMLUnit.setSAXParserFactory("org.apache.xerces.jaxp.SAXParserFactoryImpl");
 XMLUnit.setIgnoreWhitespace(true);
}

private Filter[] getFilters(){
 return new Filter[] {
 new RegexPackageFilter("java|org"),
 new SimplePackageFilter("junit.")
 };
}

private Dependency[] getDependencies(){
 return new Dependency[] {
 new Dependency("com.vanward.resource.XMLizable"),
 new Dependency("com.vanward.xml.Element")
 };
}
}
```

Running these tests becomes a simple matter of defining the proper Ant targets for running each group. For example, to run all tests belonging to the unit group, the TestNG Ant task has a group attribute that can take a comma-separated String of group names:

```xml
<target name="testng-unit" depends="testng-init">
  <mkdir dir="${testng.output.dir.unit}"/>

  <testng groups="unit"
          outputDir="${testng.output.dir.unit}"
          sourceDir="${testng.source.dir}"
          classpath="${testclassesdir};${classesdir}">

    <classfileset dir="${testng.source.dir}">
      <include name="**/*Test.java"/>
    </classfileset>
    <classpath>
      <path refid="build.classpath"/>
    </classpath>

  </testng>
</target>
```

As you can see, TestNG facilitates test categories quite effectively—that's one of this framework's selling points and an interesting influence on the newest version of JUnit.

4.5 Summary

Implementing a categorization strategy for developer tests is fairly easy, as long as the team commits to a common mechanism. Running these categories at various intervals within a CI strategy then becomes a simple matter of calling the proper build target. Dig it?

4.6 References

TestNG   http://www.testng.org
JUnit   http://www.junit.org
DbUnit   http://dbunit.sourceforge.net/
JWebUnit http://jwebunit.sourceforge.net/
XMLUnit   http://xmlunit.sourceforge.net/

Chapter 5

Spring AOP

by Stuart Halloway

Stuart is a founding partner at Relevance, LLC.

Prior to founding Relevance, Stuart was chief architect at Near-Time and the chief technical officer at DevelopMentor. Stuart is the author of Component Development for the Java Platform, part of the DevelopMentor book series and available for free online.

Stuart writes regularly, including a long-running column for the Java Developer Connection and articles for JavaPro magazine and InformIT. Stuart regularly speaks at industry events including the No Fluff, Just Stuff Java symposiums, Pragmatic Studio: Ajax, and JavaOne. Prior to DevelopMentor, Stuart worked as a lead engineer and project manager, shipping successful projects for Prentice Hall, National Geographic, and Duke University's Humanities Computing Facility. He received his B.S. and M.P.P. from Duke University in 1990 and 1994, respectively.

Aspect-oriented programming (AOP) is the unsung other core of Spring. Although dependency injection (DI) deserves its place as the core of Spring, the combination of DI and AOP is more powerful than the sum of its parts. This chapter introduces Spring AOP in the belief that AOP should be a standard part of all modern Spring development.

We will introduce the core concepts of AOP, show how they work hand-in-hand with DI, and present sample code to demonstrate each point along the way. At the conclusion, we will look at changes in Spring 2 that may make AOP both easier to use and more powerful.

5.1 From Java to Dependency Injection to AOP

Java is not just an application platform—it is a platform for writing *components*, reusable modules of software. Probably the key feature in Java that encourages reuse is the use of interface. An interface, unlike a class, implies no specific implementation. Instead, an interface is simply a list of required methods. When you program in terms of interfaces, you can easily introduce new components. No recompilation is required, as long as the new components continue to honor existing interfaces. To take a simple example, consider the MessageSource interface:

```
package di;

public interface MessageSource {
  public String getMessage();
}
```

Clients that need a MessageSource can program against this interface and retrieve messages. Clients do not need any knowledge of (or dependency on!) specific MessageSource interfaces. Maybe the messages come from files, from email, or from extraterrestrials. It simply does not matter. This is shown in Figure 5.1, on the next page.

Unfortunately, the use of the interface keyword is not enough to maintain a clean separation between components. For a variety of reasons, components can become *tightly coupled*, with unnecessary dependencies on internal details of other components. This defeats the intention of programming against interfaces! In Java, the following factors typically introduce tight coupling:

- Variables that are typed to concrete types.

- Calls to new.

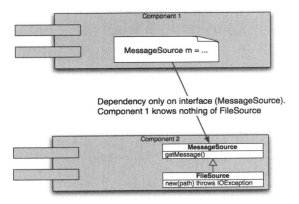

Figure 5.1: DEPENDENCY ONLY ON MESSAGESOURCE

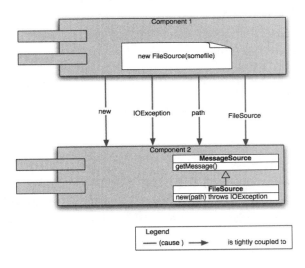

Figure 5.2: TIGHT COUPLING

- Checked exceptions.

- Statically typed argument lists for object creation. Constructors often (but not always) cause this problem.

Tight coupling is shown in Figure 5.2.

dependency injection

Plain Old Java Objects

Spring solves tight coupling with dependency injection (DI). With DI, application code takes the form of Plain Old Java Objects (POJOs). These POJOs hold interface-based references to the other objects they depend on, but they take no active role in acquiring these objects. Instead, these dependencies are managed via a configuration file and injected automatically by the container (Spring). For example, consider:

```
package di;

public interface MessageRenderer {
  public void render();
}
```

and

```
package di;

import org.springframework.beans.factory.xml.XmlBeanFactory;
import org.springframework.core.io.FileSystemResource;

public class DemoCI {
  public static void main(String[] args) {
    XmlBeanFactory bf =
        new XmlBeanFactory(new FileSystemResource("config/demo_ci.xml"));
    MessageRenderer renderer =
        (MessageRenderer) bf.getBean("renderer");
    renderer.render();
  }
}
```

The application DemoDI and the bean it calls are connected only by the MessageRenderer interface. Thanks to DI, there are no subtle forms of tight coupling to trouble us later. This is shown in Figure 5.3, on the next page.

Spring is best known for DI, which eliminates a lot of unnecessary tight coupling. But what about *necessary* coupling? You will often find a large set of dependencies among components, even with DI. Sometimes these dependencies are not clearly captured and localized in a single *cross-cutting concerns* source file. Such dependencies are called cross-cutting concerns. Here are a few examples:

- Since Java has single inheritance for implementation, it may be difficult to model entities that seem to need multiple inheritance. Secondary categorization hierarchies may have their code spread among many classes.

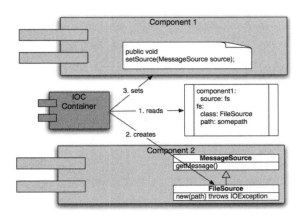

Figure 5.3: DEPENDENCY INJECTION

- Generic services, such as persistence, transactions, validation, and auditing, are typically spread across many classes.

For an example of cross-cutting concerns, consider Figure 5.4, on the following page. This shows two totally different application domains (superheroes and software projects). Within those domains, there are several classes whose instances have names. In the superhero domain, these classes all share a common base, but in software projects, they do not. Imagine that you make an application- or organization-wide change to how names are validated. This change might be easy to describe: "Our new web forms tool needs us to allow null values, which were formerly forbidden." However, the implementation change will be spread across several source code files in different application repositories. Name validation is a cross-cutting concern.

Aspect-oriented programming (AOP) allows us to localize the handling of cross-cutting concerns. Rather than having name validation spread across many classes, a name validation aspect captures everything in one place, and the run-time *weaves* the necessary code into affected classes, as shown in Figure 5.5, on the next page. *Aspect-oriented programming*

AOP and DI are complementary and synergistic. DI helps you eliminate unnecessary dependencies, and AOP helps you to localize and manage real dependencies. Together, DI and AOP are the core of Spring.

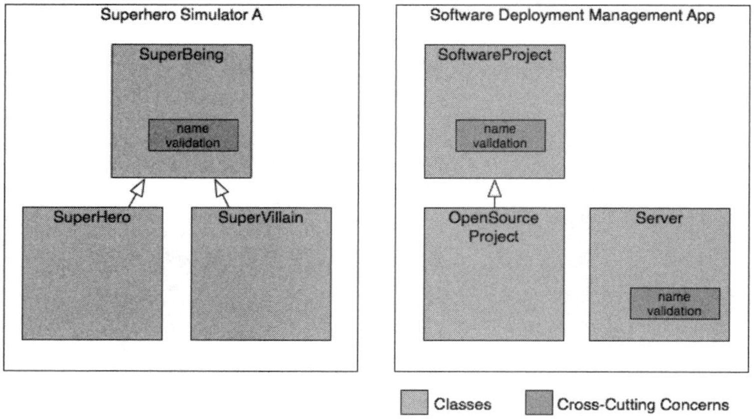

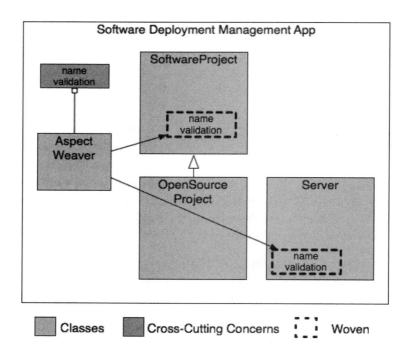

Figure 5.4: CROSS-CUTTING CONCERNS

Figure 5.5: ASPECT-ORIENTED PROGRAMMING

5.2   Aspect Terminology

In order to read the code examples that follow, you will need to know the following key AOP terms:

Term	Definition
Advice	Code that is woven in (to a pointcut)
Joinpoint	Point in the execution of an application
Pointcut	Combination of join points used to place advice
Aspect	Advice + pointcut
Introduction	Special case of advice: add entirely new fields/methods

Spring provides several approaches for wiring all this together. The sections *Advice* and *Pointcuts* will show you how to wire aspects in code, and then the section *Aspect Dependency Injection* will show you how to do the same things declaratively, using DI for your aspects. The examples shown here are representative but by no means exhaustive. Note that Spring offers more than shown here, including a number of conveniences for common tasks, plus support for many less common tasks.

5.3   Advice

Advice is code that is to be woven into existing classes. In Spring, it is possible to use advice without a pointcut, in which case the advice is woven into all methods on a bean. An example will make this clear. Consider the Superhero class:

```java
package aop;

import java.lang.reflect.Method;

public class Superhero {
  private String name;

  public String getName() {
    return name;
  }

  public void setName(String name) {
    this.name = name;
  }
}
```

We want to modify Superhero so that a null name will be rejected. The NullBlocker class will do the trick:

```java
package aop;

import org.springframework.aop.MethodBeforeAdvice;

import java.lang.reflect.Method;

public class NullBlocker implements MethodBeforeAdvice {
  public void before(Method method, Object[] objects, Object object)
      throws Throwable {
    if ((method.getName().startsWith("set")) && (objects[0] == null)) {
      throw new IllegalArgumentException("null passed to " + method.getName());
    }
  }
}
```

NullBlocker implements the class MethodBeforeAdvice, which means that it should be executed before any methods on a bean. Its sole method, before(), has a generic signature (using Method and Object arguments), because we cannot know in advance what kind of bean the NullBlocker will be applied to.

To weave this all together, we can use Spring's ProxyFactory, as shown in the following test code:

```java
package aop;

import org.springframework.aop.framework.ProxyFactory;
import util.TestBase;

public class TestBeforeAdvice extends TestBase {
  public void testBeforeAdvice() {
    Superhero h = new Superhero();
    ProxyFactory pf = new ProxyFactory();
    pf.addAdvice(new NullBlocker());
    pf.setTarget(h);
    Superhero proxy = (Superhero) pf.getProxy();
    proxy.setName("Spiderman");
    assertEquals("Spiderman", proxy.getName());
    assertThrows(IllegalArgumentException.class, proxy, "setName", (Object)null);
  }
}
```

TestBeforeAdvice demonstrates the basic steps for wiring together an aspect in Spring:

1. Create a ProxyFactory.

2. Call setTarget() to associate a POJO.

3. Call getProxy() to return an instance that has the POJO functionality, but with the Aspect woven in.

In TestBeforeAdvice, the call to the method assertThrows shows that the Superhero instance is now protected by a NullBlocker.

Many people wonder, "Wouldn't it be easier to just add the validation to Superhero directly?" If all superheroes need this validation and no other types need it, then maybe. But if the concern is cross-cutting, then others need the validation as well, and the aspect approach simplifies the code. TestBeforeAdvice2 shows the NullBlocker being used in a totally different application domain:

```
package aop;

import util.TestBase;
import org.springframework.aop.framework.ProxyFactory;

public class TestBeforeAdvice2 extends TestBase {
  public void testBeforeAdvice() {
    OpenSourceProject osp = new OpenSourceProject();
    ProxyFactory pf = new ProxyFactory();
    pf.setTarget(osp);
    pf.addAdvice(new NullBlocker());
    OpenSourceProject proxy = (OpenSourceProject) pf.getProxy();
    proxy.setName("Spring");
    assertEquals("Spring", proxy.getName());
    assertThrows(IllegalArgumentException.class, proxy, "setName", (Object) null);
  }
}
```

The advice shown in the previous two examples is called *before advice*, because it runs before the method. Before advice has access to method parameters and can prevent the execution of the method by throwing an exception. There are several other types of advice, shown in Figure 5.6, on the following page.

The interaction of the various types of advice with a method call on a Java object are shown in Figure 5.7, on the next page.

Around advice is the most powerful, because it has complete access to a method both before and after execution. This allows potent modification to existing programs. Consider the Recorder class. Recorder does a bit of gymnastics with getters and setters to keep a record of all setters called on an object. With a bean aspected by Recorder, you can get a list of past values for any bean property.

Type of Advice	AOP Alliance Interface (Spring Class)	Example Usage
Around	MethodInterceptor	Recording
Before	BeforeAdvice	Validation
Throws	ThrowsAdvice	Remapping exception types
After	AfterReturning	Remapping return types
Introduction	IntroductionInterceptor, DelegatingIntroductionInterceptor	Mixins

Figure 5.6: THE DIFFERENT TYPES OF ADVICE

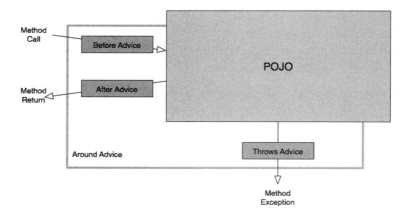

Figure 5.7: ADVICE

```
package aop;

import org.aopalliance.intercept.*;
import java.lang.reflect.Method;
import java.util.*;
import java.util.concurrent.CopyOnWriteArrayList;

public class Recorder implements MethodInterceptor {
  private List history = new CopyOnWriteArrayList();
  public Iterator historyIterator() {
    return history.iterator();
  }
  public Method getterForSetter(Class cls, Method m) {
    String name = m.getName();
    if (name.startsWith("set")) {
      try {
        return cls.getMethod(name.replaceFirst("set", "get"));
      } catch (NoSuchMethodException e) { ; }
    }
    return null;
  }
  public Object invoke(MethodInvocation mi)
      throws Throwable {
    Method method = mi.getMethod();
    Method getter = getterForSetter(mi.getThis().getClass(), method);
    Object result = null;
    if (getter != null) {
      Object before = getter.invoke(mi.getThis());
      result = mi.proceed();
      if (before != getter.invoke(mi.getThis())) {
        history.add(new Record(method.getName(), before));
      }
    } else {
      result = mi.proceed();
    }
    return result;
  }
  public static class Record {
    private final String method;
    private final Object value;
    public boolean equals(Object o) {
      if (this == o) return true;
      if (o == null || getClass() != o.getClass()) return false;

      final Record record = (Record) o;
      if (!method.equals(record.method)) return false;
      if (value != null ? !value.equals(record.value) : record.value != null)
          return false;

      return true;
    }
```

```
public int hashCode() {
  int result;
  result = method.hashCode();
  result = 29 * result + (value != null ? value.hashCode() : 0);
  return result;
}

public Record(String method, Object value) {
  this.method = method;
  this.value = value;
}
  }
}
```

The TestRecorder class demonstrates the Recorder in action.

```
package aop;

import util.TestBase;
import org.springframework.aop.framework.ProxyFactory;
import static aop.Recorder.*;

public class TestRecorder extends TestBase {
  public void testRecorder() {
    ProxyFactory pf = new ProxyFactory();
    Recorder r = new Recorder();
    pf.addAdvice(r);
    pf.setTarget(new Superhero());
    Superhero hero = (Superhero) pf.getProxy();
    hero.setName("Spiderman");
    assertIteratorEquals(r.historyIterator(), new Record("setName", null));
    hero.setName("Batman");
    assertIteratorEquals(r.historyIterator(),
                         new Record("setName", null),
                         new Record("setName", "Spiderman"));
  }
}
```

Although this Recorder is pretty simple, the implications are powerful. Similar code could be used to audit all access, record all state changes into persistence media, implement undo and redo, or perform a variety of other services around managing object state.

Recorder is written as around advice because it needs access to the method before it runs (to cache the old value of a property) and after it runs (to check whether the property changed). The other forms of advice (before, after, and throws) provide subsets of around behavior. It is considered good style to use the weakest advice that can get the job done. Don't use around advice unless none of the simpler types will do.

5.4 Pointcuts

The advice examples were applied to all methods on a bean. Often, it is necessary to limit the application of advice to some methods and not others. Spring AOP provides several ways to create such pointcuts:

- You can configure static pointcuts based on the names of methods or classes, by simple name matching or by regular expression.

- You can configure dynamic pointcuts that examine the runtime call stack to determine where to apply advice. This is used less often, since examining the call stack is expensive.

- The entire pointcut architecture is built around interfaces (but of course!), so you can define your own pointcuts if Spring's provided ones do not match your needs.

The basic steps to using pointcuts in Spring are as follows:

1. Start with one or more POJOs.
2. Write some advice.
3. Write some pointcuts.
4. Combine pointcuts and advice into an advisor (advisor is another name for Aspect).
5. Use the ProxyFactory to weave the advisor and the POJOs together.

As an example, let's start with a slightly larger POJO, PersonName:

```
package aop;

public class PersonName {
  private String lastName;
  private String firstName;
  private String middleInitial;
  public String getLastName() {
    return lastName;
  }
  public void setLastName(String lastName) {
    this.lastName = lastName;
  }
  public String getFirstName() {
    return firstName;
  }
  public void setFirstName(String firstName) {
    this.firstName = firstName;
  }
  public String getMiddleInitial() {
    return middleInitial;
  }
}
```

```
    public void setMiddleInitial(String middleInitial) {
      this.middleInitial = middleInitial;
    }
}
```

We want to make sure that PersonName's fields are not set to null. The NullBlocker we wrote earlier can be reused here. But this time there is a twist: first names and last names cannot be null, but middle initials can. The TestNameMatchMethodPointcut class demonstrates how:

```
package aop;

import util.TestBase;
import org.springframework.aop.framework.ProxyFactory;
import org.springframework.aop.support.*;
import org.springframework.aop.Advisor;

public class TestNameMatchMethodPointcut extends TestBase {
  public void testNameMatchMethodPointcut() {
    ProxyFactory pf = new ProxyFactory();
    NameMatchMethodPointcut pc = new NameMatchMethodPointcut();
    pc.setMappedNames(new String[]{"setLastName", "setFirstName"});
    Advisor adv = new DefaultPointcutAdvisor(pc, new NullBlocker());
    pf.addAdvisor(adv);
    pf.setTarget(new PersonName());
    PersonName pn = (PersonName) pf.getProxy();
    assertThrows(IllegalArgumentException.class, pn, "setFirstName", (Object) null);
    assertThrows(IllegalArgumentException.class, pn, "setLastName", (Object) null);
    pn.setMiddleInitial(null);
  }
}
```

NameMatchMethodPointcut is part of Spring, and it matches an array of names. There are several methods for setting the names to match; here we call setMappedNames(). The constructor for DefaultPointcutAdvisor then combines our pointcut and advice into an advisor. Calling addAdvisor() configures the ProxyFactory, and then we use getProxy() to retrieve our aspected PersonName.

For more complex situations, you can use JdkRegexpMethodPointcut to match classes and methods by regular expression, as demonstrated by the method TestJdkRegexpMethodPointcut:

```
package aop;

import util.TestBase;
import org.springframework.aop.framework.ProxyFactory;
import org.springframework.aop.support.*;
import org.springframework.aop.Advisor;
```

```
public class TestJdkRegexpMethodPointcut extends TestBase {
  public void testIt() {
    ProxyFactory pf = new ProxyFactory();
    JdkRegexpMethodPointcut pc = new JdkRegexpMethodPointcut();
    pc.setPattern("aop.*set.*Name");
    Advisor adv = new DefaultPointcutAdvisor(pc, new NullBlocker());
    pf.addAdvisor(adv);
    pf.setTarget(new PersonName());
    PersonName pn = (PersonName) pf.getProxy();
    assertThrows(IllegalArgumentException.class,
        pn, "setFirstName", (Object) null);
    assertThrows(IllegalArgumentException.class,
        pn, "setLastName", (Object) null);
    pn.setMiddleInitial(null);
  }
}
```

Note that this code is almost the same as the previous example, except for the line that creates the pointcut. Beware that with regular expression pointcuts, the regular expression must match the fully qualified class name plus the method name.

5.5 Aspect Dependency Injection

As we have seen, creating an aspected bean is a matter of wiring POJOs, advice, and pointcuts together. Most Spring applications will not do this wiring in application code, instead preferring to configure aspects via dependency injection. The TestDeclarativeAop class demonstrates creating a PersonName bean with aspects injected:

```
package aop;

import util.TestBase;
import org.springframework.context.ApplicationContext;
import org.springframework.context.support.FileSystemXmlApplicationContext;

public class TestDeclarativeAop extends TestBase {
  public void testIt() {
    ApplicationContext ac =
        new FileSystemXmlApplicationContext("config/test_declarative_aop.xml");
    PersonName pn = (PersonName) ac.getBean("personName");
    assertThrows("IllegalArgument", pn, "setFirstName", (Object) null);
    assertThrows("IllegalArgument", pn, "setLastName", (Object) null);
    assertDoesNotThrow(pn, "setMiddleInitial", (Object) null);
  }
}
```

But hold on a minute—there is nothing in TestDeclarativeAop that says anything about aspects! The fact that the PersonName bean uses (or does not use) aspects is an implementation detail. In fact, if you could see aspects in TestDeclarativeAop, then we would have an unnecessary dependency on aspects, which is exactly the kind of thing DI helps us avoid. To see that Spring AOP is being used, you would have to look at the bean configuration file:

```xml
<?xml version="1.0" encoding="UTF-8"?>
<!DOCTYPE beans PUBLIC "-//SPRING//DTD BEAN//EN"
        "http://www.springframework.org/dtd/spring-beans.dtd">

<beans>
  <bean id="personName"
        class="org.springframework.aop.framework.ProxyFactoryBean">
    <property name="target">
      <bean class="aop.PersonName"/>
    </property>
    <property name="interceptorNames">
      <list>
        <value>nullNameBlocker</value>
      </list>
    </property>
  </bean>
  <bean id="nullNameBlocker"
        class="org.springframework.aop.support.DefaultPointcutAdvisor">
    <property name="advice">
      <bean class="aop.NullBlocker"/>
    </property>
    <property name="pointcut">
      <bean class="org.springframework.aop.support.JdkRegexpMethodPointcut">
        <property name="pattern">
          <value>aop.*set.*Name</value>
        </property>
      </bean>
    </property>
  </bean>
</beans>
```

Here you can see that personName is not declared as a PersonName at all. Instead, personName is a Spring ProxyFactory. The target property then specifies the actual PersonName POJO, and the interceptorNames property contains a list of advisors. The personName bean has only one advisor, the nullNameBlocker.

If you examine its bean properties, you will see that it contains advice (a NullBlocker) and a pointcut (a JdkRegexpMethodPointcut with an appropriate pattern). With this configuration file, the TestDeclarativeAop application is the DI equivalent of the TestJdkRegexpMethodPointcut app shown previously.

Note that the target and pointcut properties use nested beans. Another alternative would have been to make these top-level named beans in their own right, and then refer to them by reference. The choice of nested beans is an important decision, because it indicates our intent that these beans are not to be used alone but only in the context of the top-level beans personName and nullNameBlocker. Keeping the list of top-level beans small makes it easy for clients to find the beans they need, without wading through all the subsidiary support beans.

There is an even more important reason for making target (the raw PersonName POJO) a nested bean. If the raw PersonName could be accessed directly, its first and last names could be set to null. On the other hand, the pointcut might reasonably be used elsewhere, so the choice between top-level and nested bean for pointcut is not nearly so clear-cut. As a rule of thumb, beans that require their aspects in order to function correctly should be nested inside their ProxyFactory.

5.6 Spring 2

Note: The following is based on the most recent build available at the time of this writing: the March 6, 2006, Spring 2 M3 daily build. Some details may change.

Spring 2 makes several important enhancements in the area of aspects:

- Spring 2 uses XML Schema (xsd) instead of Document Type Declarations (DTDs) to describe the bean configuration file. This, in turn, allows a new AOP-specific namespace to be introduced. The new AOP namespace provides a cleaner, terser syntax for aspects.

- Spring 2 allows the use of AspectJ's pointcut language, which is *AspectJ* much more powerful (and complex) than Spring AOP.

- Spring 2 allows Aspects to be POJOs, instead of forcing them to have dependencies on interfaces such as MethodBeforeAdvice and MethodInterceptor.

In addition to all this new goodness, the Spring team is determined to provide an easy transition path from Spring AOP up to AspectJ. To this end, all the 1.*x* features continue to work.

Better still, the new AOP namespace uses Aspect terminology directly, instead of referring to Spring-specific classes. This lets you plug in different implementations with no other change to configuration. New

applications can use the new configuration schema to start simple with
Spring AOP and then power up to the AspectJ pointcut language with
a minimum of fuss. The TestDeclarativeAop application demonstrates
AOP, Spring 2–style:

```
package aop2;

import org.springframework.context.support.FileSystemXmlApplicationContext;
import org.springframework.context.ApplicationContext;
import aop.PersonName;
import util.TestBase;

public class TestDeclarativeAop extends TestBase {
  public void testIt() {
    ApplicationContext ctxt =
        new FileSystemXmlApplicationContext("config/test_declarative_aop_2.xml");
    PersonName pn = (PersonName) ctxt.getBean("personName");
    assertThrows("IllegalArgument", pn, "setFirstName", (Object) null);
    assertThrows("IllegalArgument", pn, "setLastName", (Object) null);
    assertDoesNotThrow(pn, "setMiddleInitial", (Object) null);
  }
}
```

By now it should come as no surprise that this client shows no awareness that it depends on beans that use aspects (or Spring 2, for that
matter). To look under the hood, check out the configuration file:

```
<?xml version="1.0" encoding="UTF-8"?>
<beans xmlns="http://www.springframework.org/schema/beans"
       xmlns:xsi="http://www.w3.org/2001/XMLSchema-instance"
       xmlns:aop="http://www.springframework.org/schema/aop"
       xsi:schemaLocation="http://www.springframework.org/schema/beans
               http://www.springframework.org/schema/beans/spring-beans.xsd
               http://www.springframework.org/schema/aop
               http://www.springframework.org/schema/aop/spring-aop.xsd">

  <aop:config>
    <aop:aspect id="nullBlocker" ref="paramValidator">
      <aop:pointcut id="pc"
                    expression="execution(* set*Name(..)) and args(name)"/>
      <aop:before pointcut-ref="pc"
                  method="blockNull"
                  arg-names="name "/>
    </aop:aspect>
  </aop:config>
  <bean id="personName"    class="aop.PersonName"/>
  <bean id="paramValidator" class="aop2.ParamValidator"/>
</beans>
```

Here things are quite a bit different. First you see a bunch of schema
and namespace goo added as attributes on the <beans> element. This

is verbose but boilerplate. Then the fun begins. The aop:config element configures our aspect. Much of this is self-explanatory. Here are a few key points:

- The aspect specifies not only an aspect instance paramValidator, but also the exact method and arguments that will be called (the method and arg-names() attributes). This is a necessary good. Since paramValidator is now a POJO, we can choose to invoke any method we want as before advice.

- The expression attribute uses the AspectJ pointcut syntax. That's a topic for a whole book, but suffice it to say that this matches calls of the form setXXXName() and makes the argument available to the aspect.

Now let's look at ParamValidator:

```java
package aop2;

public class ParamValidator {
  public void blockNull(String name) {
    if (name == null) {
      throw new IllegalArgumentException("Cannot be null");
    }
  }
}
```

The important thing here is what's not here. ParamValidator is just a POJO—no aspects or Spring-specific interfaces. Since we can invoke any method on this POJO as advice, we have chosen the meaningful name blockNull. (This hints that in the future we might hang all sorts of other advice methods on this same class.)

The sum of these new features is very exciting. The new configuration syntax and POJO support make aspects more friendly and approachable and may encourage wider adoption. On the other end of the scale, the AspectJ integration makes Spring AOP much more powerful and ready to tackle more complex problems. With Spring 2, aspects have completed their move from "esoteric power tool" to a regular part of the development process for all applications.

5.7   In Conclusion

Spring represents the tireless application of common sense and field-tested knowledge to Java development. The two cores of Spring are dependency injection (DI) and aspect-oriented programming (AOP).

With DI, you rid your code of unnecessary dependencies—it becomes focused, testable, and domain-oriented. With AOP, you can elegantly manage the necessary dependencies in your application. Your application source files can each clearly focus on a single task and avoid degeneration to an unmaintainable tangle of cross-cutting concerns.

5.8 Resources

Sample Code Download

The Spring Exploration application sample code used in this article is available online at http://www.codecite.com/project/spring_xt. Some of the examples were inspired by *Pro Spring* [HM05], which is recommended follow-up reading.

Running the Code

The code was tested against the following classpath on an M3 build of Spring 2. All the code before the Spring 2 section was also tested on Spring 1.2.6. You would use the same JAR files on 1.2.6, minus the "asm" files.

Classpath

```
eclipse/plugins/org.junit_3.8.1/junit.jar
spring-framework-2.0-m3/dist/spring.jar
spring-framework-2.0-m3/lib/asm/asm-2.2.1.jar
spring-framework-2.0-m3/lib/asm/asm-analysis-2.2.1.jar
spring-framework-2.0-m3/lib/asm/asm-attrs-2.2.1.jar
spring-framework-2.0-m3/lib/asm/asm-commons-2.2.1.jar
spring-framework-2.0-m3/lib/asm/asm-tree-2.2.1.jar
spring-framework-2.0-m3/lib/asm/asm-util-2.2.1.jar
spring-framework-2.0-m3/lib/asm/asm-xml-2.2.1.jar
spring-framework-2.0-m3/lib/aspectj/aspectjweaver.jar
spring-framework-2.0-m3/lib/cglib/cglib-nodep-2.1_3.jar
spring-framework-2.0-m3/lib/jakarta-commons/commons-logging.jar
spring-framework-2.0-m3/lib/log4j/log4j-1.2.13.jar
```

Recommended Books

- *Pro Spring* [HM05] by Rob Harrop and Jan Machacek

- *AspectJ in Action* [Lad03] by Ramnivas Laddad

Utility Code

Utility code that is called by the examples in this article is included here for reference:

```java
package util;

import junit.framework.TestCase;

import java.lang.reflect.Method;
import java.lang.reflect.InvocationTargetException;
import java.util.*;

public class TestBase extends TestCase {
  static final HashMap exTypes = new HashMap();
  static {
    exTypes.put("IllegalArgument", IllegalArgumentException.class);
  }
  private Method getMethod(Object o, String methName, Object... args) {
    Class cls = o.getClass();
    Method[] methods = cls.getMethods();
    for (int i = 0; i < methods.length; i++) {
      Method method = methods[i];
      if (method.getName().equals(methName)) {
        return method;
      }
    }
    throw new IllegalArgumentException(String.format("%s has no %s",
                                                     cls, methName));
  }
  public void assertIteratorEquals(Iterator it, Object... value) {
    int count=0;
    while (it.hasNext()) {
      assertEquals(value[count], it.next());
      count++;
    }
    assertEquals(count, value.length);
  }
  public Object assertDoesNotThrow(Object obj, String meth,
                                   Object... args) {
    Method method = getMethod(obj, meth, args);
    try {
      return method.invoke(obj, args);
    } catch (IllegalAccessException e) {
      throw new Error(e);
    } catch (InvocationTargetException e) {
      throw new Error(e.getTargetException());
    }
  }
  public void assertThrows(String exPrefix, Object obj, String meth,
                           Object... args) {
```

```java
      Class cls = (Class) exTypes.get(exPrefix);
      if (cls == null) {
        throw new Error("Unknown exPrefix " + exPrefix +
                         ", add to exTypes");
      }
      assertThrows(cls, obj, meth, args);
    }
    public void assertThrows(Class exClass, Object obj, String meth,
                             Object... args) {
      Method method = getMethod(obj, meth, args);
      try {
        method.invoke(obj, args);
      } catch (InvocationTargetException ite){
        Throwable t = ite.getTargetException();
        if (!exClass.isAssignableFrom(t.getClass())) {
          throw new Error(t);
        }
        return;
      } catch (IllegalAccessException e) {
        fail("Unexpected " + e);
      }
      fail("Expected " + exClass);
    }
  }
```

Chapter 6

Dependency Management

by Kirk Knoernschild

Kirk is chief technology strategist at QWANtify, where he leads based on his firm belief in the pragmatic use of technology. In addition to his work on large development projects, Kirk shares his experiences through developing courseware, teaching, writing, and speaking at seminars and conferences. Kirk has provided training to thousands of software professionals, teaching courses on UML, Java J2EE technology, object-oriented development, component-based development, software architecture, and software process.

As CTS at QWANtify, Kirk works with clients and peers to develop high-quality software that solves real business challenges. In addition to spending a good share of his time on projects, Kirk's role typically involves mentoring other developers on proven coding and design techniques and driving QWANtify's technology vision. He intimately understands the software life cycle, and has applied many best practices espoused by industry-proven agile methodologies, such as the Rational Unified Process and Extreme Programming.

Kirk is the author of Java Design: Objects, UML, and Process [Kno01]. He frequently contributes to various technical publications and actively updates his personal website with new articles and white papers on a variety of software development topics. He is also the founder of Extensible Java, a growing resource of design pattern and dependency management heuristics.

Kirk's favorite book and favorite tool selections are on page 218.

6.1 Dependency Defined

Why is software so difficult to change? When you establish your initial vision for the software's design and architecture, you imagine a system that is easy to modify, extend, and maintain. Possibly, you envision system modules that are reusable not only within the system but also across systems. Unfortunately, as time passes, changes trickle in that exercise your design in unexpected ways. Unlike what you had anticipated, each change begins to resemble nothing more than another hack, until finally the system becomes a tangled web of code that few developers care to venture through.

Eventually, modifications to the software that are intended to improve the application have the opposite effect: they break other parts of the system. The software is beginning to rot. The most common cause of rotting software is tightly coupled code with excessive dependencies. In this chapter, we'll explore some common symptoms of rotting design due to excessive dependencies, examine their cause, and present solutions that can be used to minimize dependencies between classes, packages, and binary units of deployment.

A dependency can be defined as follows:

If changing the contents of a module M2 may impact the contents of another module, M1, we can say that M1 has a Dependency on M2.[1]

class dependency

package dependency

physical dependency

In Java, there are three modules where dependencies exist. A class dependency exists when one class has a relationship to another class. A package dependency exists when a class in one package imports a class in another package. A physical dependency exists when the contents of one deployable unit, or .jar file, uses the contents of another deployable unit.

In Figure 6.1, on the next page, we see that class Client imports the Service class from package service, where Client is deployed in client.jar and Service is deployed in service.jar. This simple example illustrates the three different types of dependencies. The first is a class dependency between class Client and class Service. The second is a package dependency between package client and package service, and the third is a physical dependency between client.jar and service.jar.

---

[1] (*Java Design: Objects, UML, and Process* [Kno01])

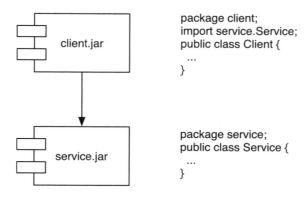

```
package client;
import service.Service;
public class Client {
    ...
}
```

```
package service;
public class Service {
    ...
}
```

Figure 6.1: CLASS, PACKAGE, AND PHYSICAL DEPENDENCY

Understanding dependencies between modules provides valuable information about the structural makeup of your software system. For instance, we know that changes to class Service may impact class Client. Changes to package service may impact package client, and changes to any of the contents of service.jar may impact the contents of client.jar. Of course, for any interesting software system, some dependencies are necessary. But dependencies should be minimized, and techniques are available to help us manage and break complex dependencies.

6.2 Dependency Challenges

Managing dependencies is about minimizing coupling between modules. Excessive dependencies challenge developers in numerous ways:

- *Dependencies hinder the maintenance effort.* When you're working on a system with heavy dependencies, you typically find that changes in one area of the application trickle to many other areas of the application. In some cases, you cannot avoid this. For instance, when you add a column to a database table that must be displayed on a page, you'll be forced to modify at least the data access and user interface layers. Such a scenario is mostly inevitable. However, applications with a well-thought-out dependency structure should embrace this change instead of resisting it. Applications with complex dependencies do not accommodate change well. Instead, with change, the system breaks in unexpected ways and in unexpected places. For this to happen, the module you unexpectedly broke must be dependent on the module that changed.

- *Dependencies prevent extensibility.* The goal of object-oriented systems is to create software that is open for extension but closed to modification. This idea is known as the Open-Closed Principle (see *Java Design: Objects, UML, and Process* [Kno01]). The desire is to add new functionality to the system by extending existing abstractions, and plugging these extensions into the existing system without making rampant modifications. One reason for heavy dependencies is the improper use of abstraction, and those cases where abstractions are not present are areas that are difficult to extend.

- *Dependencies inhibit reusability.* Reuse is often touted as a core advantage of well-designed OO software. Unfortunately, few applications realize this benefit. Too often, we emphasize class-level reuse. To achieve higher levels of reuse, we must carefully consider the package structure and deployable unit structure. Software with complex package and physical dependencies minimizes the likelihood of achieving higher degrees of reuse.

- *Dependencies restrict testability.* Tight coupling between classes eliminates the ability to test classes independently. Unit testing is a fundamental principle that should be employed by all developers. Tests provide you with the courage to improve your designs, knowing mistakes will be caught by unit tests. They also help you design proactively and discourage undesirable dependencies. Heavy dependencies discourage independent testing of software modules.

- *Dependencies limit understanding.* When you work on a software system, it's important that you understand the system's structural architecture and design constructs. A structure with complex dependencies is inherently more difficult to understand.

Dependencies between different types of modules have different effects on your design and architecture. Complex class dependencies may not be troublesome if they are confined to a single package or deployable unit. Yet if these classes are heavily used throughout the application, are used across applications, or are part of a framework or class library, the dependencies will cause problems. Package dependencies aren't necessarily bad if they are confined to a single unit of deployment, but if package dependencies span units of deployment, reconsidering the package structure to minimize the coupling between packages will prove beneficial. Physical dependencies may not cause problems unless you need to independently reuse a deployable unit. If the module is heavily dependent on one or more other modules, reuse is a burden. In the next few sections, we discuss in more detail the dependencies between various modules and explore ways that dependencies can be minimized and eliminated.

6.3   Class Dependencies

Class dependencies are relationships between classes dictated by your code. A class declared as an instance variable, passed as a parameter, or defined locally within a method creates an associative relationship between the containing class and the declared class. Extending an abstract class or implementing an interface also creates a static relationship between the descendant and ancestor. When developing object-oriented software systems, dependencies are created through either inheritance or association. If you're familiar with Unified Modeling Language (UML), you're aware of the distinction between association, aggregation, and composition. When managing dependencies, each of these is treated as an equal.

Inheritance is a static relationship between two classes where one, the descendant, is an extension of another, the ancestor. In Java, inheritance manifests itself in one of two ways. Using the extends keyword, a class inherits the operations and behavior of its base class. Conversely, using the implements keyword, a class inherits only the operations defined on an interface. Arguably, implementation inheritance using the extends keyword is worse. Implementation inheritance exists when the purpose for extension is to reuse functionality defined within the ancestor. A significant concern with implementation inheritance is that it's a static, compile-time relationship offering no flexibility for extension. You cannot change your ancestors. Let's see an example.

In Figure 6.2, on the following page, Descendant extends Ancestor where Ancestor defines a simple method named reuse(). The reuse() method can easily be overridden or accessed by all future descendants of Ancestor. The problem is that all future descendants of Ancestor always receive the same implementation of reuse and do not have the ability to easily change the method behavior based on system state.

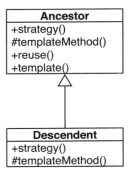

Figure 6.2: INHERITANCE IS A STATIC RELATIONSHIP

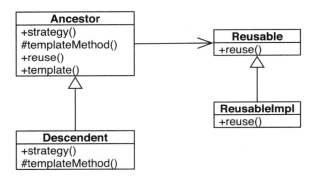

Figure 6.3: ASSOCIATION IS A DYNAMIC RELATIONSHIP

Although you cannot change your ancestors, you can easily change who you associate with. This makes association a much friendlier relationship. In Figure 6.3, the Ancestor reuse method delegates to the Reusable hierarchy. This delegation allows for Descendant to be easily configured with variations of the reuse() method, serving to minimize the dependency of Descendant on the Ancestor.reuse() method.

In addition to minimizing the dependency between the Descendant and Ancestor functionality, we have also increased the testability of Descendant. Whereas in Figure 6.2 the descendant could not be tested independently of Ancestor, we can now create mock objects and substitute these mocks anywhere descendants of Reusable are expected.

Although association is the most effective way to reduce dependencies, there are some forms of association that we should avoid. Bidirectional associations present a greater burden because each class has a reference to the other. In the diagram that follows, we see a bidirectional association between Bill and Customer. The accompanying code shows that the Customer has a list of Bill instances, while the Bill has a reference to Customer that is used to help calculate the discount applied to an individual Bill. Bidirectional associations are burdensome. Any changes to Bill impact Customer, and vice versa. Neither class can be tested independent of the other. Certainly, there must be a better way.

```
┌─────────────┐ 1        * ┌─────────────┐
│  Customer   ├───────────┤    Bill     │
└─────────────┘           └─────────────┘
```

```java
public class Customer {
  private List bills;
  public BigDecimal getDiscountAmount() {
    ...code...
  }
  public List getBills() {  return this.bills;  }
  public void createBill(BigDecimal chargeAmount) {
    Bill bill = new Bill(this, chargeAmount);
    ...code...
  }
}

public class Bill {
  private BigDecimal chargeAmount;
  private Customer customer;
  public Bill(Customer customer,
              BigDecimal chargeAmount) {
    this.customer = customer;
    this.chargeAmount = chargeAmount;
  }
  public BigDecimal pay() {
    BigDecimal discount = new BigDecimal(1).
    subtract(this.customer.getDiscountAmount()).
    setScale(2, BigDecimal.ROUND_HALF_UP);
    //make the payment...
    return paidAmount;
  }
}
```

It's possible to replace the bidirectional associations with a unidirectional one. In this example, Customer depends on Bill, but Bill has no knowledge of Customer:

This is a step in the right direction. Bill can now be tested and maintained independently of Customer. However, another interesting problem has arisen. Whereas in the bidirectional example the Bill class contained the knowledge required to calculate the discount, the client of Bill (in this case our test) must pass the discount amount to the pay method, requiring clients of Bill to calculate this discount amount. We have sacrificed ease of use to minimize the dependency structure. Wouldn't we rather have the best of both worlds?

```java
public class Customer {
  private List bills;
  public BigDecimal getDiscountAmount() {
    ...code...
  }
  public List getBills() {  return this.bills;  }
  public void createBill(BigDecimal chargeAmount) {
    Bill bill = new Bill(chargeAmount);
    ...code...
  }
}

public class Bill {
  private BigDecimal chargeAmount;
  public Bill(BigDecimal chargeAmount) {
    this.chargeAmount = chargeAmount;
  }
  public BigDecimal getChargeAmount() {
    return this.chargeAmount;
  }
  public BigDecimal pay(BigDecimal discountAmount) {
    //make the payment...
    return paidAmount;
  }
}
```

Avoiding the disadvantages of a bidirectional association is important. So too is making your classes easy to use and understand by exposing a clear, concise interface. One useful way to break a bidirectional association is to introduce an abstraction that guarantees a unidirectional compile-time relationship while accommodating a bidirectional run-time relationship. How do we do this?

Figure 6.4, on the next page, introduces a DiscountCalculator interface. The code for the DiscountCalculator interface is trivial and not shown. The Customer class implements DiscountCalculator, allowing Customer to pass itself as a DiscountCalculator type to Bill when Bill is instantiated. The code for this version of Bill is now virtually identical to the code for the previous Bill. The significant difference is that Bill now references the

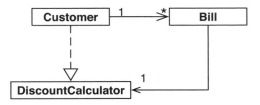

Figure 6.4: ABSTRACT ASSOCIATION

DiscountCalculator interface instead of the Customer class.

The class diagram in Figure 6.4 illustrates this relationship. Analyzing the dependency structure, we find that Bill is independent of the Customer class, offering us the advantages of a unidirectional relationship while also ensuring the Bill interface remains clean. Additionally, the system is more extensible since we can easily create new implementations of DiscountCalculator when necessary. Testing is also aided since we can continue to test Bill independently of Customer by simply defining a mock implementation of DiscountCalculator, allowing us to focus our testing efforts only on the Bill class. A true unit test!

```java
public class Customer implements DiscountCalculator {
  private List bills;
  public BigDecimal getDiscountAmount() {
    ... code ...
  }
  public List getBills() {    return this.bills;    }
  public void createBill(BigDecimal chargeAmount) {
    ... code ...
  }
}

public class Bill {
  private BigDecimal chargeAmount;
  private DiscountCalculator discounter;
  public Bill(DiscountCalculator discounter,
            BigDecimal chargeAmount) {
    this.discounter = discounter;
    this.chargeAmount = chargeAmount;
  }
  public BigDecimal pay() {
    BigDecimal discount = new BigDecimal(1).
        subtract(this.discounter.getDiscountAmount()).
        setScale(2, BigDecimal.ROUND_HALF_UP);
    BigDecimal paidAmount = this.chargeAmount.
        multiply(discount).setScale(2);
```

```
        //make the payment...
        return paidAmount;
    }
}
```

Minimizing coupling between classes is a good design decision. A flexible way to minimize coupling is to use abstractions to help break complex compilation dependencies. This promotes other good practices, such as increasing testability. Many common design patterns are based upon using abstractions to manage dependencies and create extensible designs. This idea, known as *abstract coupling*, is central to managing dependencies among packages and the binary units of deployment, as well.

6.4 Package Dependencies

If class dependencies are dictated by code, then package dependencies are driven by the relationships between classes that span packages. As we've seen, bidirectional relationships between classes are an unwise design choice in many cases because of the increased coupling. Managing dependencies among packages is driven by a similar idea. When designing packages, we want to avoid all cycles in the dependency structure. Cycles in the dependency structure exist when we can trace the package relationships and end with the package from which we started.

Cycles

Figure 6.5, on the facing page shows our resulting class structure with a default allocation to their respective packages. Customer and Discount-Calculator both reside in the cust package, while Bill resides in the bill package. Although there are no bidirectional relationships between classes, there is a cyclic dependency between the cust and bill packages.

Although cyclic dependencies between packages are not always bad, allowing such cycles to overtake your application is not good design. Cycles between packages, especially if complex, make managing class relationships more difficult. If you are certain that there are no cyclic package relationships, you can be certain there are no bidirectional class relationships that span packages. As we'll see, eliminating cyclic package dependencies is the first step toward a flexible physical structure. But first, let's explore how to break package cycles and then make certain cycles don't resurface.

The package cycle in Figure 6.5, on the next page, is relatively easy to break. Simply moving the DiscountCalculator class from the cust package

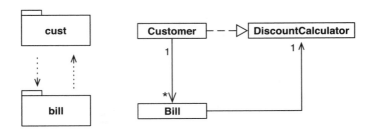

Figure 6.5: CYCLIC PACKAGE RELATIONSHIPS

to the bill package, as shown in Figure 6.6, on the following page, eliminates the cycle. In *Large-Scale C++ Software Design* [Lak96], Lakos refers to this as a callback, since at run-time Bill is passed a reference *callback* to a Customer as the DiscountCalculator type, and proceeds to call back into Customer when needed. Callbacks are one very good technique for minimizing dependencies and breaking cycles between both packages and the units of deployment. Two other techniques from Lakos are escalation, where the dependency is pushed to a class in a higher- *escalation* level package or .jar file, and demotion where the dependency is pushed *demotion* down. An example of Escalation is how the dependency was initially broken between Customer and Bill by breaking the bidirectional association, though at the risk of making the client more complex. Common examples of escalation include mediator and control classes, and one of the risks is a more complex, centralized behavioral structure. Pushing the calculation down to a concrete DiscountCalculator class would have been an example of demotion, though doing so in this situation would have been counterproductive.

Escalation, demotion, and callbacks each have their preferred uses. Escalation should be used when the code causing the dependency controls the relationship. Escalated code is typically not functionality that you have a strong desire to reuse. On the other hand, demotion is most useful when the code is common functionality that is reused, and callbacks are most useful when you need well-defined points of extension within the application.

In many cases, eliminating cycles between packages is simply a matter of moving code, not necessarily modifying code. This is especially the case if you stay current on managing package dependencies. Let a

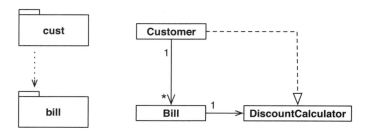

Figure 6.6: ACYCLIC PACKAGE RELATIONSHIPS

number of cyclic dependencies creep into your application, and breaking the cyclic structure will become much more complex.

It was simple to the break the package cycle by moving DiscountCalculator. This illustrates an important design principle. *Interfaces and abstract classes should be closer to the classes that use them than they are to the class that implements or extends them.* Because descendants are dependent on their ancestor, not vice versa, placing the ancestor closer to the class dependent on it allows us to work miracles when managing dependencies. We'll explore these wonders more when discussing physical dependencies, so you'll have to wait a few minutes.

On large applications, with potentially hundreds of packages, it can quickly become difficult to understand and manage package relationships. Using JDepend, you can write unit test cases to verify the package structure, and you can incorporate JDepend into your Ant build script, giving you a report that shows package dependencies. The following listing shows a simple JDepend test case:

JDepend

code/kirkk/DependencyConstraintTest.java

```java
package com.kirkk.test;

import junit.framework.*;
import junit.textui.*;
import jdepend.framework.*;

public class DependencyConstraintTest extends TestCase {
    private JDepend jDepend;

    public static void main(String[] args) {
        junit.textui.TestRunner.run(DependencyConstraintTest.class);
    }
```

```
    public DependencyConstraintTest(String name) {
        super(name);
    }


    protected void setUp() throws Exception {
        PackageFilter filter = new PackageFilter();
        filter.addPackage("java.*");
        jDepend = new JDepend(filter);
        jDepend.addDirectory("build/com/kirkk/cust");
        jDepend.addDirectory("build/com/kirkk/bill");
    }

    public void testPackageDependencies() {
        DependencyConstraint constraint = new DependencyConstraint();

        JavaPackage cust = constraint.addPackage("com.kirkk.cust");
        JavaPackage bill = constraint.addPackage("com.kirkk.bill");

        cust.dependsUpon(bill);
        jDepend.analyze();
        assertEquals("Dependency Mismatch", true,
                        jDepend.dependencyMatch(constraint));

    }

    public void testCycles() {
        java.util.Collection packages = jDepend.analyze();
        assertEquals("Cycles exist", false, jDepend.containsCycles());
    }
}
```

The setup() method begins by filtering all packages beginning with java to exclude them from the output. We then add all directories containing the classes we want to analyze. Since JDepend is a byte code utility and is not classpath-dependent, we need to include in the directory name the fully qualified package name, as well.

The testPackageDependencies() method verifies that the only existing dependency constraints are the ones it defines. In our case, we state that the cust package depends only on the bill package. No other package dependencies should exise. This test method would pass for the structure in Figure 6.6, on the preceding page, but would fail for the structure in Figure 6.5, on page 97. The testCycles() method analyzes all packages and determines whether any cyclic dependencies exist among the package defined in the test's setup() method. Again, in our case, the test would fail if run from the design in Figure 6.5 but would pass for the design in Figure 6.6.

JDepend can also be incorporated into your Ant build script to provide an HTML report that shows, among many other things, the dependencies between packages. The next listing shows an excerpt from an Ant build script that defines a JDepend target. The first section specifies that we will use the JDepend Ant task to analyze our build directory. For reference, the build directory being analyzed should be the directory containing the compiled .class files. This produces an XML document which is formatted using the JDepend.XSL style sheet to produce a much nicer-looking HTML document. I'll leave it as your exercise to produce a JDepend report to see what it looks like. It's worth your while, and if you already have a repeatable build script available, adding JDepend will take only a few minutes. If you don't have a repeatable build script, use this as motivation to create one. You'll find it worthwhile. Better yet, set up an automated build, and include JDepend as a report on your build website.

`code/kirkk/Ant_snippet.xml`

```xml
<target name="jdepend" depends="compile">
  <jdepend format="xml" outputfile="${buildstats}/jdepend.xml">
    <classespath>
      <pathelement location="${build}" />
    </classespath>
    <classpath location=""/>
  </jdepend>

  <style in="${buildstats}/jdepend.xml" out="${buildstats}/jdepend.html"
         style="${lib}/jdepend.xsl">
  </style>
</target>
```

6.5 Physical Dependencies

Binary dependencies are the relationships between packages that span the units of deployment. Many of the techniques used to manage and minimize physical dependencies can also be used to manage package dependencies, and vice versa. More so than with package dependencies, cycles between the units of deployment is not a wise design decision. Such cycles eliminate independent reuse potential, complicate deployment, and hinder maintenance. Whereas limited cycles in the package structure may not prove too costly, cycles among the units of deployment are never good.

Fortunately, we have many ways to break physical dependency cycles, and techniques exist that will help restructure the physical relation-

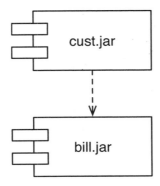

Figure 6.7: ALLOCATION TO UNITS OF DEPLOYMENT

ships. As we saw in Figure 6.6, on page 98, the Customer class resides in the cust package, and the Bill and DiscountCalculator classes reside in the bill package.

Let's assume for a moment that the cust package is deployed in cust.jar and the bill package is deployed in bill.jar, resulting in the component diagram in Figure 6.7.

What if, for example, we were not concerned with the reuse of bill.jar but instead were more concerned with reusing cust.jar? In the previous scenario we cannot deploy cust.jar without bill.jar, causing potentially unnecessary overhead. We want to decouple cust.jar from bill.jar. What we want to do, then, is invert the relationship between bill.jar and cust.jar, yielding the structure shown in Figure 6.8, on the next page. But how can we do this?

We invert the relationship between packages or units of deployment by introducing an abstraction in the appropriate place. To eliminate the cyclic relationship between packages in Figure 6.5, on page 97, we moved DiscountCalculator from the cust package to the bill package. Here, however, we do not have an existing abstraction that can be moved. Instead, we need to introduce a new abstraction.

In Figure 6.9, on the next page, we have refactored the Bill class to an interface, placing it in the cust package. We then introduce DefaultBill, which is the implementation from the former Bill class. Since the Bill interface now resides in the cust package, the relationship from bill to cust has been eliminated, as has the dependency from cust.jar to bill.jar.

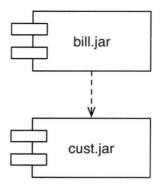

Figure 6.8: INVERTING PHYSICAL DEPENDENCIES

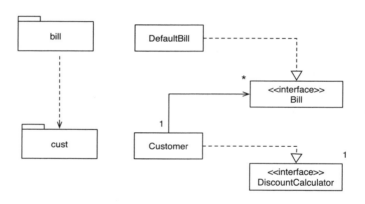

Figure 6.9: REFACTORED CLASS STRUCTURE

Since DefaultBill implements the Bill interface, the direction of the relationship has changed since descendants are dependent on their ancestors. DefaultBill depends on Bill, and the relationship between packages, and subsequently between bill.jar and cust.jar, has been inverted.

While inverting the relationship provides us with the ability to deploy and reuse cust.jar separately from bill.jar, we have increased the dependencies of bill.jar. It's possible we want bill.jar and cust.jar to be independent of each other while still using the services of each other at runtime. Is it possible to completely eliminate compile-time relationships while maintaining the run-time relationships? Yes! It's easy.

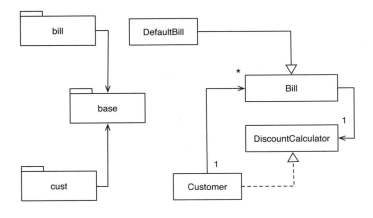

Figure 6.10: REALLOCATING CLASSES

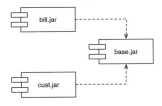

Figure 6.11: ELIMINATING PHYSICAL DEPENDENCIES

In Figure 6.10, we have introduced a new package named base, moving the DiscountCalculator and Bill interfaces to this new package. After refactoring Bill to an interface, the Customer and DefaultBill classes have no compile-time dependency, making these two classes completely independent of each other. By simply moving the abstractions to the base package (neither closer to nor farther from the classes using them or realizing them), we have eliminated the relationship between the cust and bill packages, as well. Consequently, if we deploy the base package in base.jar, cust.jar and bill.jar are no longer dependent on each other. Instead, both are dependent on base.jar, as shown in Figure 6.11.

When designing package relationships, we saw that JDepend can be used to help verify and maintain the integrity of your package designs. However, JDepend cannot be used to manage the relationship between .jar files. Instead, we must turn to two other techniques.

levelized build

A levelized build is a componentized compile. Instead of compiling the entire application, you choose to compile a single .jar file, starting with the .jars that have no outgoing application dependencies, and including only the minimum necessary in the classpath for each .jar you compile. As you can guess, a levelized build is possible only if no cyclic physical dependencies exist. If cycles did exist, it would be difficult to determine which .jar file was lowest in the hierarchy of .jars. Assuming your structure is acyclic, a levelized build will enforce your physical structure. Failed builds will weed out undesirable dependencies. The listing that follows shows a snippet of a low-grade levelized build used to build the .jar files in Figure 6.11, on the preceding page. Many of the trivial targets have been omitted. Note that the basecompile target includes only the source directory in the classpath since the base.jar file we are compiling has no external dependencies. On the other hand, the billcompile target includes base.jar in its classpath. These specific classpaths enforce the physical dependency structure. Any undesirable dependencies will cause the build to fail.

code/kirkk/levelized_build.xml

```xml
<project name="Comp" default="analyzerdot" basedir=".">
  <target name="basecompile" depends="init">
    <mkdir dir="${buildsrc}"/>
    <mkdir dir="${build}"/>
    <copy todir="${buildsrc}">
      <fileset dir="${src}">
        <include name="com/kirkk/base/**"/>
      </fileset>
    </copy>
    <javac srcdir="${buildsrc}" destdir="${build}">
      <classpath>
        <pathelement path="${buildsrc}"/>
      </classpath>
    </javac>
    <jar jarfile="${dist}/base.jar"
         basedir="${build}"
         includes="com/kirkk/base/**"/>
    <copy todir="${classes}">
      <fileset dir="${build}">
        <include name="**/*.class"/>
      </fileset>
    </copy>
    <delete dir="${buildsrc}"/>
    <delete dir="${build}"/>
  </target>

  <target name="billcompile" depends="basecompile">
    <mkdir dir="${buildsrc}"/>
```

```
    <mkdir dir="${build}"/>
    <copy todir="${buildsrc}">
      <fileset dir="${src}">
        <include name="com/kirkk/bill/**"/>
      </fileset>
    </copy>
    <javac srcdir="${buildsrc}" destdir="${build}">
      <classpath>
        <pathelement path="${buildsrc}"/>
        <pathelement path="${dist}/base.jar"/>
      </classpath>
    </javac>
    <jar jarfile="${dist}/bill.jar"
        basedir="${build}"
        includes="com/kirkk/bill/**"/>
    <copy todir="${classes}">
      <fileset dir="${build}">
        <include name="**/*.class"/>
      </fileset>
    </copy>
    <delete dir="${buildsrc}"/>
    <delete dir="${build}"/>
  </target>
</project>
```

But what if you have an existing project that you know has a number of cyclic physical dependencies? You cannot use a levelized build because the structure must be acyclic. JDepend can be used only to find cyclic package dependencies. JarAnalyzer is a utility that can be used to help *JarAnalyzer* identify cyclic physical dependencies. JarAnalyzer parses a directory of .jar files and identifies the dependencies between them.

JarAnalyzer is strictly a post-compile tool with two different output formats. The first uses .xml to provide a detailed description of the contents of a .jar file, including any cycles in the dependency structure. The second uses GraphViz and DOT to generate a visual component diagram showing the relationships between .jar files. Running JarAnalyzer using GraphViz and DOT as part of the build in the previous listing would yield the diagram in Figure 6.11.

The following listing illustrates two targets that incorporate JarAnalyzer into the build script in the previous build.xml script. The analyzerxml target generates XML output, while the analyzerdot target uses GraphViz and DOT to generate a visual component diagram showing the relationships between .jar files.

`code/kirkk/analyzer.xml`

```
<target name="analyzerxml" depends="jdepend">
  <taskdef name="jaranalyzer"
           classname="com.kirkk.analyzer.textui.JarAnalyzerTask">
    <classpath>
      <pathelement path="${lib}/jaranalyzer-0.9.3.jar"/>
      <pathelement path="${lib}/bcel-5.1.jar"/>
      <pathelement path="${lib}/jakarta-regexp-1.3.jar"/>
      <pathelement path="${lib}"/>
    </classpath>
  </taskdef>
  <jaranalyzer srcdir="${dist}"
               destfile="${buildstats}/dependencies.xml"
               summaryclass="com.kirkk.analyzer.textui.XMLUISummary" />
</target>

<target name="analyzerdot" depends="analyzerxml">
  <taskdef name="jaranalyzer"
           classname="com.kirkk.analyzer.textui.JarAnalyzerTask">
    <classpath>
      <pathelement path="${lib}/jaranalyzer-0.9.3.jar"/>
      <pathelement path="${lib}/bcel-5.1.jar"/>
      <pathelement path="${lib}/jakarta-regexp-1.3.jar"/>
      <pathelement path="${lib}"/>
    </classpath>
  </taskdef>

  <jaranalyzer srcdir="${dist}"
               destfile="${buildstats}/dependencies.grph"
               summaryclass="com.kirkk.analyzer.textui.DOTSummary" />
  <exec executable="dot" >
    <arg line="-Tpng -Nshape=box -Nfontsize=30 -Nwidth=1.5 -Nheight=1.25
               ./stats/dependencies.grph -o ./stats/dependencies.png"/>
  </exec>
</target>
```

6.6 Conclusion

Developers spend time designing class relationships, whether using Big Design Up Front (BDUF) or a more agile approach such as Test Driven Development (TDD). Regardless of approach, if you think only about your class structure, you risk compromising the structural integrity of the application. You should also give careful consideration to the package structure and physical structure. Although you may not always opt for the more powerful solution, an awareness of techniques to manage dependencies between these higher-level modules is critical. Software with well-managed dependencies is ultimately more flexible, extensible, maintainable, and testable. That is a Good Thing.

Chapter 7

Process Choreography and the Enterprise Service Bus

by Mark Richards

Mark Richards is certified senior IT architect at IBM, where he is involved in the architecture and design of large-scale service-oriented architectures in J2EE and other technologies, primarily in the financial services industry. He has been involved in the software industry as a developer, designer, and architect since 1984 and has significant experience and expertise in J2EE architecture and development, object-oriented design and development, and systems integration. Mark served as the president of the Boston Java User Group in 1997 and 1998 and the president of the New England Java Users Group from 1999 through 2003, where he helped grow the group from its original 30 members to more 2700, earning the recognition as one of the top 25 Java User Groups in the world. Mark is an IBM Certified Application Architect, a Sun Certified J2EE Business Component Developer, a Sun Certified J2EE Enterprise Architect, a Sun Certified Java Programmer, a BEA WebLogic Certified Developer, and a Certified Java Instructor. He holds a master's degree in computer science from Boston University. He has spoken at several conferences around the country, including the No Fluff, Just Stuff symposium, Boston Java Users Group, New England Java Users Group, Maine Java Users Group, and other professional groups and conferences.

Mark lists his favorite books and tools starting on page 218.

7.1 Introduction

In my NFJS session titled "The Role of the Enterprise Service Bus (ESB)," I define an ESB by the many capabilities it could have. Two of those capabilities are service orchestration and process choreography. In this chapter I expand on these topics and describe the relationship and interaction between process choreography, service orchestration, and the enterprise service bus.

service orchestration

process choreography

When we move to a service-oriented architecture (SOA) we have the opportunity to make a proper distinction between business services and implementation services. A business service is a service that the end user or business sponsor understands and defines, whereas an implementation service is something a developer designs, codes and implements. Typically a business service is defined as an interface that contains a service name, input specification, and output specification. One way to define a business service in SOA is through WSDL (Web Services Definition Language). Business services are usually much courser-grained than implementation services and reflect the nature of the business rather than how business processes are technically implemented.

business service

implementation service

By contrast, an implementation service is a function or method that a developer codes and implements using the specifications defined in the business service. The specifications for an implementation service may or may not be the same as those for the business service. An implementation service may need additional information (i.e., security credentials) that are required for implementation but not for the business specification. The ability to define business processes through services and not have them tied directly to how they are implemented is one of the main benefits of SOA.

To understand this concept, consider an example of a trading firm that deals in the exchange of securities. The specific business rules and procedures that the firm uses are defined through business services (i.e., WSDL) and implemented through implementation services (i.e., Java methods). If the firm wants to replace its custom trading application with a third-party solution, it should not have to redefine the way it does business, and it should not have to redefine its business services; it should be a purely technology task. The business services describe the business and should remain independent of the underlying technology and implementation (making them more static), whereas the implementation services change with respect to the platform, vendor, and technology advances (making them more dynamic). The relationship between the enterprise service bus and these service types is that the ESB is the abstraction layer that binds business services to implementation services.

7.2 Process Choreography vs. Service Orchestration

The reason why the distinction between a business service and implementation service is important is that it provides a clear and concise definition between process choreography and service orchestration. Simply stated, process choreography is the coordination of multiple business services, whereas service orchestration is the coordination of implementation services.

Process choreography is typically implemented through an XML-based language called BPEL (Business Process Execution Language). Vendors (and open source projects) create process servers that execute BEPL *process servers* and coordinate business services. By contrast, service orchestration is typically implemented through interservice communication, through aggregate services within the implementation layer, or sometimes even through the ESB.

For example, in the securities trading firm described previously, the following business services are defined for creating a new trade order, placing a trade with a broker, and executing a trade:

- CreateTradeOrder
- PlaceTrade
- ExecuteTrade

Each of these business services maps to one or more corresponding implementation services as follows:

CreateTradeOrder   OrderService.validateOrder( ), OrderService.create( )
PlaceTrade   TradingService.createPlacement( )
ExecuteTrade   TradingService.executeTrade( )

Notice how the CreateTradeOrder business service maps to more than one implementation service, whereas the other business services have a one-to-one mapping with the corresponding implementation service. Also notice that the names of the corresponding services do not necessarily have to match. Figure 7.1 illustrates this relationship.

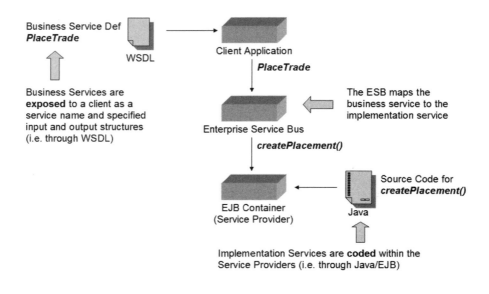

Figure 7.1: BUSINESS VS. IMPLEMENTATION SERVICES

For equity securities (i.e., common stock), each of the business services listed previously are invoked independently. However, for fixed-income securities (i.e., corporate bonds, treasury notes, etc.), the placement and execution of the trade is typically executed all at once in a single request. Therefore, to handle this business request let's define one more business service called PlaceFixedIncomeTrade. Notice that the following mappings for this business service are other business services, not implementation services:

PlaceFixedIncomeTrade   PlaceTrade
                         ExecuteTrade

Through process choreography the PlaceTrade and ExecuteTrade business services would be executed and coordinated as a single request. From the client's perspective it is a single request, but from the process perspective it is two business service requests coordinated as one.

7.3   ESB

From an architecture standpoint there are four main components that make up the capabilities of an ESB:

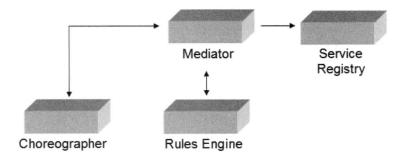

Figure 7.2: ESB COMPONENTS

- Mediator
- Service Registry
- Choreographer
- Rules Engine

The Mediator is the primary component and is typically the main entry *Mediator* point into the ESB. It handles most of the capabilities of an ESB, including routing, communication, message processing, message and protocol transformation, message enhancement, error handling, transaction management, and security. The Service Registry handles the service *Service Registry* mappings that link the business service to the corresponding implementation service. The Choreographer handles process choreography *Choreographer* (the coordination of multiple business services for a single business request such as PlaceFixedIncomeTrade discussed previously). The Rules Engine component communicates with the Mediator component to pro- *Rules Engine* cess any rules-based message enhancement or routing requests. Figure 7.2 illustrates the relationship between the components that make up an ESB.

7.4 ESB and Process Choreography Relationship

The component used as the entry point into the ESB must be able to handle message processing, transaction management, and security. These capabilities are typically managed by the Mediator component. The message-processing capability refers to the ability of the ESB to manage request state and to ensure guaranteed delivery of the response message to the client. The transaction control capability refers to the coordination of resources and data integrity aspects of the request. The security capability refers to the authentication, authorization, and auditing that must be handled in an SOA environment. Given the ESB component architecture described previously, we have three possible design approaches for defining the relationship between the Choreographer and the Mediator:

Choreographer Below Mediator
> *Client → Mediator → Choreographer*

Choreographer Above Mediator
> *Client → Choreographer → Mediator*

Choreographer and Mediator at Same Level
> *Client → Choreographer or Mediator*

No single product can effectively provide all the capabilities of an ESB. Therefore, even vendors with bundled ESB offerings generally provide separate products that make up the ESB that correspond to the architecture components discussed earlier. Most vendor ESB offerings have the flexibility to define any one of these design approaches. I will go into details of each approach, explain the implications of each design, and describe why having choreography below the Mediator is the best design approach.

7.5 Choreographer Below Mediator (Recommended)

In this design approach the client communicates with the Mediator component of the ESB, regardless of whether process choreography is needed. The Mediator component, seeing that process choreography is needed, then transfers control to the process choreographer. Otherwise, the Mediator communicates directly with the service provider (i.e., Java object). The three primary capabilities of the entry point component (message processing, transaction control, and security) are handled by the Mediator. This design approach is based on the assumption that, for most enterprise architectures, process choreography does not account for the majority of requests made to an ESB. The diagram in Figure 7.3, on the next page, illustrates this design approach.

As you can see from Figure 7.3, the client application always communicates with the ESB through the Mediator. The Mediator accepts the request and communicates with the Service Registry to get the ser-

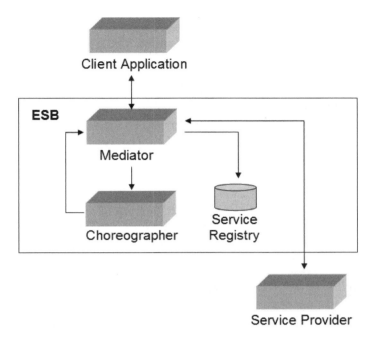

Figure 7.3: CHOREOGRAPHER BELOW MEDIATOR

vice mappings. To the Mediator the Choreographer component is just another service destination.

Process Flow

Here's how a request involving process choreography is processed using our PlaceFixedIncomeTrade example:

1. First, the client executes a PlaceFixedIncomeTrade business service request. The Mediator accepts the request via HTTP or MQ, performs authentication and authorization, and starts a "relaxed ACID" transaction or activity scope.

2. The Mediator asks the Service Registry for the location of the PlaceFixedIncomeTrade business service. The Service Registry returns the address and port number of the corresponding implementation service, which in this case happens to point to the message queue or HTTP address used by the Choreographer.

3. The Mediator sends a message to the Choreographer to process the PlaceFixedIncomeTrade business service. The Choreographer receives the request and executes the BPEL for the PlaceFixedIncomeTrade business service.

4. There are two BPEL nodes for the PlaceFixedIncomeTrade request: PlaceTrade and ExecuteTrade. The Choreographer executes the first BPEL node containing the PlaceTrade business service by sending the request to the Mediator in the same way an external client would. Notice in this case the Choreographer acts as a client to the Mediator.

5. The Mediator receives the PlaceTrade business service request via HTTP or MQ from the Choreographer, performs authentication and authorization, and starts a "relaxed ACID" transaction (or activity) scope in the same manner as the original request.

6. The Mediator asks the Service Registry for the location of the PlaceTrade business service. The Service Registry returns the address and port of the corresponding implementation service, which in this case happens to point to the createPlacement() method of the TradingService EJB.

7. The Mediator either sends a message or directly invokes the createPlacement() method via RMI/IIOP. The method returns the result to the Mediator. The Mediator, having completed the request for PlaceTrade, returns the result to the client, which in this case is the first BPEL node in the Choreographer.

8. The Choreographer moves to the next BPEL node and executes the ExecuteTrade business request. The same process is repeated for the ExecuteTrade business service as was for the PlaceTrade business service. Once the BPEL is complete, the Choreographer sends the final results to the Mediator (the original request thread).

9. The Mediator, now having received the response from the original message sent to the Choreographer, returns the result of the PlaceFixedIncomeTrade to the client.

To summarize, the previous sequence works like this: the Mediator treats the Choreographer as just another implementation service endpoint. The Choreographer, containing business services, makes its request to the ESB via the Mediator as if it were another external client.

This simplicity is what makes this design approach so powerful and robust. There is a clear separation of responsibility between components as well as a high level of abstraction between components (i.e., the mediator does not need to know whether a service needs choreography).

This design approach has good performance characteristics because the Choreographer (which is not the fastest component on the planet) is invoked only when needed. Scalability is also good with this approach because the Mediator component is much more scalable than most process servers (BPEL engines). Finally, this design approach is much less complex than the other approaches because only those services requiring choreography are specified in BPEL and only a single component (i.e., the Mediator) is responsible for message processing, transaction control, and security.

7.6 Choreographer Above Mediator

With this design approach the client always communicates with the process server (BEPL engine), which in turn communicates with the ESB Mediator component. Unfortunately, this design approach is what is typically found in most vendor ESB solutions and architectures. The diagram in Figure 7.4, on the following page, illustrates this design approach.

As you can see from Figure 7.4, all requests from the client first enter the Choreographer, regardless of whether the request requires process choreography. As the entry point into the ESB, the Choreographer must provide the basic entry point capabilities described earlier (message processing, transaction control, and security), something some vendor process servers do not provide.

The main disadvantage to this approach is that every request, whether it needs process choreography or not, must go through the process server. This means that every business service must have a corresponding BPEL, even if it is only a single node. Not only is this inefficient, but it lacks the proper scalability provided by fast Mediator components. It also lacks the proper performance characteristics required by most applications and is more complex because every service must be defined in WSDL, BPEL, and the Service Registry. Generally speaking, business service requests processed via an ESB must be extremely fast and efficient to overcome the additional layers of abstraction put

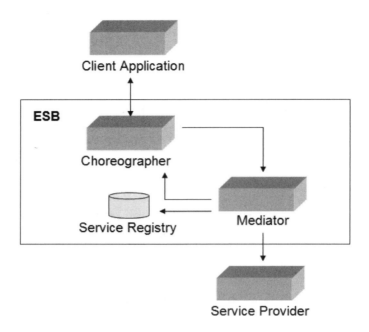

Figure 7.4: CHOREOGRAPHER ABOVE MEDIATOR

in place by SOA. I would not recommend this design approach unless 90% or more of your services require process choreography. Even then I would still consider the first design approach.

7.7 Choreographer and Mediator at same level

This design approach is a compromise between the prior two design approaches. Instead of having to choose between the Mediator and Choreographer as the ESB entry point, this design approach makes either one an entry point. Therefore, the client can choose to communicate with the Choreographer or Mediator, depending on whether process choreography is needed. Figure 7.5, on the next page, illustrates this approach.

Although this design approach may seem the most flexible, it has the most disadvantages of the three designs. As you can see from the diagram, this approach requires that both the Mediator and Choreogra-

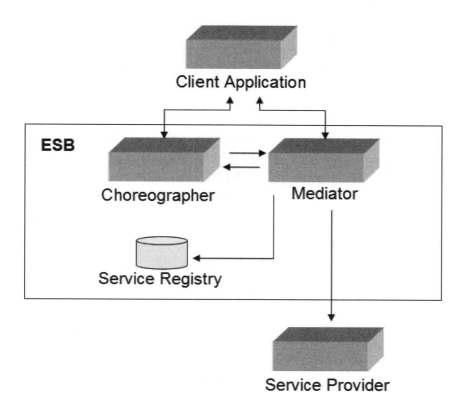

Figure 7.5: CHOREOGRAPHER AND MEDIATOR AT SAME LEVEL

pher components supply the entry point capabilities (message processing, transaction control, and security). This adds complexity and doubles the maintenance effort within the ESB. Also, this approach places the burden on the client for deciding which services require choreography and which ones do not. In this case service characteristics are not abstracted from the client, requiring modifications at the client level if a business service suddenly requires process choreography (or the other way around). Finally, this approach contains additional complexity because there is no clear separation of responsibilities between components, and component interaction is unclear and confusing.

7.8 Conclusion

Process choreography has been a source of confusion and complexity within the context of SOA and enterprise service bus design. Remembering a few simple things will help clarify some of the confusion and remove the complexity associated with this capability. First, process choreography is the coordination of business services, whereas service orchestration is the coordination of implementation services. Second, placing process choreography below the Mediator in the ESB produces a much more scalable design approach that has better performance and less complexity than other design approaches.

Chapter 8

The Cornerstone of a Great Shop

by Jared Richardson

Jared Richardson, coauthor of Ship It! A Practical Guide to Successful Software Projects [RG05], is a developer-turned-manager who thinks a good day is having everything delegated so that he can sneak away and actually write code. He specializes in using off-the-shelf technologies to solve tough problems, especially those involving the software development process.

I did a lot of lawn mowing when I was younger. My brother and I tried to make our summer money by asking real estate agents if we could mow the lawns of their absentee clients. We'd usually land one realtor each year and they'd give us enough business to keep us busy all summer. One of the lessons I learned is how hard it is to cut a straight line when you're mowing a wide yard. When I was in the middle of the yard, I felt like I was cutting a straight line, but then I would get to the end of the row and look back to discover a crooked mess. It always amazed me how something could seem so right and yet be so off-course.

8.1 Timely Feedback

A software project can be a lot like mowing a yard. Even though we try to move in a straight line, and we think we are, later we look back and are amazed at how far the project ran off-course.

Whether mowing yards or building software, we need timely feedback to help keep us on-track. Looking back at completed software projects, or lawns, shows you where you missed the mark, but by then it's usually too late, at least for the stuff we've just done. We need feedback while we're still in the midst of the work. I never found a good way to get that feedback for my lawn mowing, but I have found a guide for software projects. I use continuous integration systems to keep my projects on-track.

8.2 Continuous Integration (CI)

Mike Clark calls this type of system a "virtual build monitor." This extra team member keeps an eye on your project and lets you know when things start getting off-course. If you invest in a good automated test suite, you'll quickly catch all sorts of errors that traditionally pull good projects off-course.

The more shops I get to observe, the more I'm seeing that continuous integration plays a vital role in keeping a shop on-course. In fact, these days I'm telling people that I've learned one of the basic, fundamental principals to keep both you and your project on target.

Do you want to make your product a great one? Do you want to be the best developer you can be? Then make a solid continuous integration system a first-class member of your team and the cornerstone of your shop. A good CI system eliminates many of the problems that prevent you from working on the product, your career, and your craft.

A continuous integration system does several tasks automatically.

- Monitors your source code
- Compiles after every change
- Tests your compiled code
- Notifies the developers of problems as soon as they occur

As we move forward, keep an open mind, and try to see where each step could've helped you in the last few months. Then, when we're done, I'm going to point you to a continuous integration system that is trivial to install, easy to use, and open source to boot.

Let's look at what a continuous integration system is and why it helps so much.

8.3 The Steps of CI

Continuous integration systems all have a few common functions.

First, CI systems monitor your source. The system usually watches your source code management system (Perforce, Visual Source Safe, ClearCase, CVS, Subversion, and so on). Most systems can also monitor other resources, such as file systems. This is how the software knows it's time for a build. Every time your code changes, the CI system checks out the latest version.

Second, the software compiles your project. The system runs your existing build scripts by wrapping them in an Ant script. For this to work, you'll obviously need a scripted build. If your builds are not robust or repeatable, your CI tool will expose this flaw. It will force you to have a clean build system.

Third, CI systems test your new build. Tests are created (or wrapped) in an XUnit framework (JUnit, NUnit, HtmlUnit, jsUnit, etc.), which means you have access to dozens of test frameworks that range from unit testing to browser click-through testing. When you set up a system to run tests, people are more likely to write the tests. They'll also contribute the tests they've been hiding on their own machines.

Lastly, your CI system will notify everyone of the results. The developers or testers who just changed the code will get email telling them how long the build and test took, how many tests passed, how many failed, etc. Your system will also archive the results to a web page.

However, the publishing step is very configurable. You can publish in a variety of interesting ways beyond a standard web page. You can publish to a custom web page, XML log, email, instant messaging client, or even to a lava lamp. The publish step is an extremely flexible way of sharing your build results.

8.4 What's the Big Deal?

CI either requires or encourages several key practices. These are source code management, scripted builds, and test automation. Much of the benefit that comes from using a CI system actually comes from the foundational practices that a CI system requires.

Don't get me wrong. CI adds plenty of benefit as well. It's just that many day-to-day problems go away when you use these other practices first.

8.5 Code Management

One of the first things your CI system will do for you is make sure you have your source code organized and (I hope) into a source code management system. After all, your CI software can't watch a code tree you can't identify. The first practice CI encourages is good source code management.

This benefit will seem elementary to many people, but I've seen shops that still use network drives and .zip files. Quite a few developers still haven't discovered source code management.

Proper source code management doesn't take much time at all once you've learned how to use it. Like with any good tool, you'll save much more time than you'll spend learning to be effective with the tool.

You'll save the time you normally spend reconciling code differences by hand, not to mention rewriting the work that careless co-workers overwrite from time to time. Code collisions and lost work are common issues, but a good source code system also merges your changes for you, maintains a history for each file, and more.

If you're not using a proper source code management system, I urge you to rethink your position. It's a huge time-saver.

8.6 A Scripted Build

The second thing your CI system will require is a scripted build. Moving to this step requires a level of build automation. Fortunately, this is easy to add. Many tools, both commercial and open source, solve this problem for you. You still have to understand how to build your product, but these tools will keep you from learning the different command-line options for javac or jar on different operating systems. Look at tools such as Ant, Maven, and Rake.

Like good source code management, a scripted build provides many benefits.

For starters, your teammates aren't all busy building their own versions of the build script. Everyone needs to build, and developers, being clever, will all find a slightly different way to solve the same problem. When you have a single build script, everyone is building the same way. It's OK if someone still wants to build differently (an IDE maybe?), but they need to have the ability to build the same way that everyone else does.

Don't ignore the maintenance savings either. You'll eventually improve the build script, find a bug in it, or decide to make it faster. With a single script, you do the work one time. When everyone has his or her own build method, everyone solves the same problem repeatedly. What a waste of time!

When you build your code the same way, everyone gets the same version of the product. This means the testers report problems in the same version of the program the developers run.

Without a canonical build script, you don't always get everyone on the same page. In fact, the customers, testers, and developers often run different versions of the same product and then wonder why they can't reproduce the same issues. If you've had trouble reproducing your customers' bugs, then start here. Is everyone running the same version of the product?

8.7 Test Automation

Another practice that a CI system encourages is test automation. Writing and running tests is a huge milestone for many shops and is one of the hallmarks of a great shop. I think test automation is the core of why a CI system adds such benefit. People who recognize the benefit of automating common tasks tend to be more strategic thinkers. They automate everything possible, including building and testing, because it frees them up for more interesting work. (Of course, this doesn't eliminate manual testing, but that's another topic.)

What is an automated test?

- Binary
- Automatic
- Repeatable

Binary

A test with a binary result passes or fails unambiguously. There's no question about whether the test succeeded. Sometimes a test will return a result that requires a judgment call from a tester. The odds are good that you don't need this.

Work hard to make your tests clean and binary. Write them so they evaluate the result and tell you whether a test passed or failed.

Automatic

If the test isn't automatic, then someone has to set up an environment, start the test, click a button, or look at the results. When this happens, the test becomes interactive again. Much of the benefit of test automation is lost.

You've created a hybrid test somewhere between an interactive test and an automatic test. Instead of letting a small number of testers baby-sit a large number of tests and continually add more tests, you'll have a large number of testers looking at log files all day long. Semiautomated tests are certainly better than pure interactive testing, but they fall short of where you could be. Work hard to make your tests completely automatic, including the determination of the pass or fail status.

Repeatable

An automated test also needs to be repeatable. A good test doesn't give you different results for three out of five test runs. If your tests aren't repeatable, break the tests down into smaller tests. Eventually you'll isolate the problem area and, as a bonus, you'll have new tests created for your test suite.

Don't forget about external dependencies either. You can rebuild and restock database tables cleanly before each test run with tools such as Ant's SQL task or dbUnit (http://dbunit.sourceforge.net). A dirty database table can introduce all sorts of variation into a test run. (You may want to create a small, representative data set to load for your testing runs.)

Leverage Yourself

An automated test is a great way to leverage your experience and expertise. As an expert on your product, you probably know how to test parts of it in a way that few other people can. You can encode that knowledge in a reusable format by creating an automated test. This makes your experience available without diverting your attention. Sometimes a co-worker will run the tests; other times you will. In other cases, a program will run them.

Let these bits of your expertise exercise the product while you do other things, like go home on time or stay late to solve problems that are more interesting. These tests might run while you are coding or at home sleeping, but you are doing something else. Your tests are working in the background.

8.8 Getting Started

Sometimes people won't install a CI system because they don't have tests ready to run in the system. There are enough benefits from fast compile cycles to justify using continuous integration, so don't wait. You don't wait to see a doctor until you're not sick anymore, right? Having the CI system keep your compiles clean will free up some of the time needed to start writing tests as well.

I've also found that people are much more likely to write automated tests if they're sure the tests will be used. By providing a CI system, you have a place to house your tests and run them immediately. This is the best way I know to encourage test creation. People want to create things that are used, and this assures them the tests they create will run regularly.

The best way to get started with continuous integration is to start using an existing software package. I'm going to point you to CruiseControl on SourceForge.[1] Since version 2.3, CruiseControl comes with an

---

[1] http://cruisecontrol.sf.net/

embedded servlet engine[2] and a sample project. You can download the project and see CruiseControl running in less than five minutes. Then, to add your own project, just copy the bundled example. It's easy to get started.

The CruiseControl team has a great write-up on how to run the binary release of CruiseControl. Visit http://cruisecontrol.sf.net/, and click the Getting Started link on the left.

8.9 Conclusion

The teams that I see running smoothly and cleanly always have continuous integration in place. It's a practice I respect more and more every day.

I see this practice overshadow all others. Teams that run smoothly use continuous integration. They respect the system instead of tolerating it, and the developers treat the notifications seriously. When the system says something is broken, these teams address the problem quickly. These teams insist on CI coverage from the first day of a new product.

Other shops, even those who are using a CI system but ignoring it, are different. They live in turmoil. Heroic efforts are not the exception but the rule. In fact, these teams always seem to be running behind. They always have a crisis issue to resolve or a deadline to meet.

They work and live in a perpetual twilight of stress and problems. They've lived there so long that they think it's the only way to write software. Sadly, these teams tend to burn people out. I've been there, and it's no fun. Creating software can be a great joy—and it is, when done right. CI can't solve every problem, but it can remove several categories of problems that would otherwise clutter your day and slow you down.

If you're not using a continuous integration system, try one this week. Get a system installed, and leave it running for one month. At the end of that month, turn it off if you don't see the benefit.

Don't be surprised if you find yourself missing the system the first day it's gone. You might just become one of the developers who insists on continuous integration coverage on your new projects.

---

[2]http://jetty.mortbay.com

8.10   Resources

Continuous Integration. . .
. . . http://martinfowler.com/articles/continuousIntegration.html
Martin Fowler and Matthew Foemmel on continuous integration

CruiseControl . . . . http://cruisecontrol.sourceforge.net/
The CruiseControl home page

CI Products . . . . http://www.jaredrichardson.net/ci.html
My list of products that help with continuous integration

Scripted Build Links . . . . http://www.jaredrichardson.net/buildscripts.html
My list of links on scripting your build

Pragmatic Automation . . . . http://www.pragmaticautomation.com
Mike Clark's automation blog

Jetty . . . . http://jetty.mortbay.com/jetty/index.html
A pure-Java HTTP server and servlet container

Chapter 9

Help! I've Inherited Legacy Code!

by Jared Richardson

You can read about Jared on page 119.

9.1 Use a BAT

Many times in our careers we'll find ourselves supporting legacy code. Sometimes you accept a new job, and the legacy code is your first assignment. Maybe your company reorganizes, and an old product ends up in your lap. For whatever reason, it happens. You wanted to code something new and shiny, but instead you are now the owner of a new-to-you and completely unfamiliar block of code. The code appears to be rather intricate, and now you have to wade in.

In fact, if I can stretch the definition a bit, you can consider any code written before today to be legacy code. Have you ever tried to revisit code you wrote six months ago? It's not always as easy as you'd hope to support your own code, much less someone else's. Both situations are challenging unless you follow some basic guidelines.

The traditional approach is to start making changes while doing your best to avoid unintentional collateral damage. Unfortunately, because the code is unfamiliar, you aren't sure what's really going to happen when you change a data structure or update a variable.

Rather than blindly wandering into this minefield, let's create a plan of attack. Don't just start making changes and hope that everything still works. Instead, take aim, and hit it out of the park with a BAT.

Here's a three-pronged attack you can use to attack the problem. Build, Automate, and Test. Use this BAT for your legacy code, and create a safety net for yourself. The BAT approach will ensure that your code continues to work the way you want it to work. It quickly catches unintended side effects and helps you eliminate them.

I'd like to challenge you to look at how you handle your legacy code in light of the BAT approach. See how your day-to-day work compares and see whether you need to approach your work differently.

9.2 Build

The first problem to address is the build. It's difficult to ship and test a product unless you can reliably build it. Figure out how to cleanly build the product on your desktop, and then script the process.

Occasionally this is a nonissue, but builds usually aren't nearly as clean as they should be. Often builds run only on a single machine or in a special environment. When teams pass code from owner to owner, the build tends to accumulate extra requirements—each owner adds his or her own special case to the mix. By the time you inherit the mess there have been too many cooks in the kitchen.

A complicated build can cause an avalanche of cascading problems with the entire product.

When a task is difficult, people do it less often. When a build is difficult, people build less often. It's just human nature. The ability to run a clean build often becomes a dark art mastered by only a few people in your shop. No one wants the task because it's so difficult and painful.

Since you can't test what you haven't built, testing becomes less frequent. When people finally run their tests, they find more bugs. Infrequent testing gives bugs more time to accumulate. If you are running tests daily, you'll have only one day's worth of bugs to report. However, if you wait six months to test, you'll have a lot more issues to pin down.

So, your testing becomes burdensome. Since the testers get tired of all the work in a testing cycle, they avoid testing. Entering dozens or hundreds of bugs is boring work that no one enjoys.

Developers start to dread the testing cycle because they feel bombarded and attacked by all the bug reports. So, the developers start resenting and harassing the testers, which makes the testing cycle even more painful. It's a destructive feedback loop.

A complicated build causes problems for the entire product life cycle, so be sure your build is clean.

When anyone can build, anyone can test. Testing is run more frequently, leading to smaller groups of bug reports. Having less work to do at a time is less of a chore. Anyone will move a bucket of paint and not think twice, but ask someone to move 50 buckets and see what they say.

Your goal is to create a clean build that runs on any development machine and that is easy to maintain. Use a build scripting tool or language, such as Rake, Ant, Maven, or Nant. These high-level build languages let you focus on building your application, instead of on build, language, or platform details.

When you can build your product with a single command (such as ant all), you can move on to the next step. Be sure to test this on more than one machine.

9.3 Automate

Now that you can automatically build the product on any development machine, let's automate.

Your goal is to automate the entire build and test cycle on a clean machine with an absolute minimum of human intervention. It's not always possible to have everything completely automated, but we want to reach a place where we script anything that can be reasonably automated.

Sometimes it's easier to install and configure a supporting piece of the software than to write a script to do it automatically. Applications that you install only once are prime candidates. Things such as compilers, run-time libraries, and preexisting data sets fall into this category. Don't try to reproduce the data set that takes you two hours to recreate. However, if you can rebuild a representative data set in 30 seconds, you should build from scratch. The benefits of starting with a clean, known data set are immense, but not always practical. Don't stretch a 15-minute test run into an hour by rebuilding all your data.

Be sure to document any manual steps thoroughly and keep all the instructions around for anyone else who might want to duplicate the environment.

On the other hand, why should you sit around and watch complete builds all day long? Your time is valuable. Your IDE probably handles incremental builds and small unit test runs for you anyway. In most cases, this partial coverage is good enough. Having developers run a set of smoke tests (see the sidebar), targeting active code areas, will cover most situations.

We still need a clean build and a complete test run periodically. This is how we verify that a change didn't break the product in an unexpected way. Since smoke testing often misses these types of breaks, we need to run the entire suite fairly frequently to keep the product in the best shape possible.

Instead of asking each developer to build the entire system from scratch and then run every test available five times a day—tasks that can take quite a while—we're going to ask another computer to do that for us. Since we're tasking a computer to perform the automated build and test run, there's no reason why we can't run it more than once a week. In fact, there's no reason why this cycle can't run after every code change.

> ## What's a Smoke Test?
>
> A *smoke test* is a short collection of tests that target the areas of the code that are actively being changed. Your smoke tests don't even try to exercise the entire product. A good set of smoke tests will be rotated—they aren't permanent. When you start working on a different product area, move out the old smoke tests, and cycle in others. You can select tests from your complete testing suite tests to run in your smoke test suite. I usually just add them to an Ant target (called smoke-test) that runs selected tests.

What's the best way to set up this type of automation? The quickest and easiest way is to use a continuous integration (CI) product. A CI product watches your code, builds after each change, runs your tests, and then notifies everyone involved.

A CI system creates a fast feedback loop. When you change your code, you'll find out whether anything was broken before you forget why you made the changes. (For more information about CI systems, visit my CI page at http://www.jaredrichardson.net/ci.html)

It's all about the pace of your development. You want to keep moving forward. Revisiting code edits from last week or last month is a poor way to keep rolling. Catch and fix your problems within the hour, and keep your team moving forward.

Here's how the system works. You edit the code on your desktop until you're sure you have the feature completed or the bug fixed, so you put your changes into your source code management (SCM) system. Your continuous integration system monitors your SCM and sees that code has changed. It then checks out the product, builds it, and runs all your tests. You'll immediately get an email telling you whether the compilation and test run passed or failed.

It's a simple concept that's powerful in action.

9.4 Test

The final section of our BAT is Test. Now that our CI system is building the product and running our automated tests, we need to be sure

> ### What's a Mock Client Test?
>
> A *mock client test* isn't a special testing framework. It's a test created to ensure your basic, expected functionality doesn't break. Quite often with legacy code, you'll change something in one part of the system and not know that it affects other areas of the product. I once worked on a product where changing the communication protocol affected the GUI component layout. Your mock client tests, inside your CI system, are your insurance policy against accidental change. Test your product the way that you expect it to be used, and you'll have a solid product baseline. Add tests to cover the more interesting cases later, as you encounter them.

that our tests cover the product properly. After all, a test that doesn't validate the functionality your customer uses is pretty useless from the customer's point of view.

First, try to understand how your product is used...this can be a real challenge with a legacy product. You may even want to create a set of scenarios for customer usage. For example, you could have a scenario for creating daily reports, doing daily data imports, or adding new customers.

You may also want to have categories of users called *user personas.* You could have "Joe the Power User," "Mary the System Administrator," or "Fred the New User." Each persona uses your product differently just like a power user uses the product differently than a rank novice.

Next, create mock client tests (see the sidebar) to duplicate the most common customer usage scenarios.

A great testing strategy is *defect-driven testing.* Every time you find a bug in the system, add a new test that covers that defect. While you are adding the specific test, look for other tests you can add that are close but not quite the same. Over time, this strategy provides good coverage in the areas of the product that need coverage the most.

Regardless of how you choose to add tests, make adding tests a priority. Having a basic test suite in place is essential if you plan to make any changes to the product.

Your final step is getting the tests into your continuous integration system.

You get feedback quickly on any problems when your automated tests run in your continuous integration environment. Every time you add or change the code, you get a "from scratch" build and a complete test run. Most developers get addicted to this additional coverage quickly and soon depend on this "extra team member."

So, remember:

- Write scenarios.
- Create mock client tests.
- Use continuous integration.

9.5 Knock It Out of the Park

Build, automate, and test (BAT) is good advice for anyone writing code, but it's an especially good formula for anyone inheriting legacy code. The ability to refactor with confidence is essential. I find it difficult to be productive if I'm constantly looking over my shoulder to see what I'm breaking. A good test suite looks over my shoulder for me and lets me focus on the performance improvements I'm trying to make.

Remember, never change legacy code until you can test it, and never test purely by hand unless you have no other option.

Don't fear legacy code—handle it properly. Hit it with this BAT, and you'll win every time.

Chapter 10

Using Code Coverage to Improve Testing Effectiveness

by Ian Roughley

Ian Roughley is an independent consultant based in Boston, Massachusetts. For more than ten years he has been providing architecture, development and mentoring services to clients ranging in size from Fortune 100 companies to start-ups. His professional background includes work in the financial, insurance, pharmaceutical, retail, hospitality, e-learning, and supply-chain industries.

Focused on a pragmatic and results-based approach, he is a proponent of open source, as well as process and quality improvements through agile development techniques. Ian is a committer on the WebWork project, a Sun Certified Java Programmer, a Sun Certified J2EE Enterprise Architect, and an IBM Certified Solutions Architect.

Ian's list of favorite books and tools starts on page 219.

Eventually in every software development project, someone asks about the quality of the code. This is a hard topic to address, even on small projects. A key reason is that the quality of the code is usually associated with the code coverage result, and the code coverage result is dependent on "something else" happening. This "something else" is running and utilizing tests that specifically exercise the application code whose quality is being questioned.

Not only do the tests need to be present, but to ensure consistent code coverage results, they need to be consistent themselves. They need to be written at the same level of granularity, to be consistent in testing adverse conditions and exceptions, to consistently assert object graph results to the same depth, and even to ensure there are asserts in the testing code.

Along with these process challenges comes an emotional component. The tool gives us a code coverage percentage at the project, package, and class levels. This percentage can increase or decrease during the development of the project. In some development environments, especially under aggressive timelines, it can be easy to place blame incorrectly by taking the numbers out of context.

Given these complexities, is code coverage worth employing? In my opinion, the answer is yes. Apart from code coverage, the other main metric associated with quality is the success percentage of automated developer tests. There are problems associated with this result also. It is possible, and common, to have a 100% success rate from unit testing while testing less than 100% of the code. The big picture is available only when you combine automated testing and code coverage.

This chapter will address the issue of quality by looking at three techniques that can be used to improve testing effectiveness: using code coverage to zero in on hard-to-test code, maintaining code coverage percentage over of the life of the project, and comparing user and developer testing percentages.

10.1 Background

Cobertura

We'll focus on the open source project Cobertura.[1] This is a code coverage tool that is freely available, that is easy to configure via Ant tasks,

---

[1]http://cobertura.sourceforge.net

and that provides complete basic functionality. There are only two missing features that I would find helpful: a historical report, so the code coverage trend information over the entire development life cycle could be easily viewed; and an IDE plug-in, which would increase the use of Cobertura as a code coverage tool when developing with small development iterations. You can find these additional features in some of the many other options for code coverage tools, including commercial products.

Although Cobertura can be run from the command line, we will focus on the provided Ant tasks that allow for easy integration into automated builds. To configure Cobertura in your Ant build file, you need to add the following top-level task definition:

```
<taskdef classpathref="classpath" resource="tasks.properties"/>
```

To capture code coverage data, the code coverage application needs to access the byte code of the classes being executed. In Java applications, you have two ways to achieve this, and both involve instrumenting the byte code.

The first method uses a tool to instrument the class files after the code has been compiled. This is the simplest method and involves less run-time configuration. To make things even easier, the tools generally provide Ant tasks that can be integrated into your build environment.

The second method uses a provided class loader that will instrument the classes as they are loaded into the JVM. Although there is one less build step, the environment you are deploying to must allow you to use a custom class loader.

Cobertura uses the first method. The following Ant target instruments the byte code, producing augmented code that will collect the code coverage data:

```
<target name="instrument" depends="compile">
  <cobertura-instrument todir="${instrumented.dir}"
                        classpath="classpath">
    <ignore regex="org.apache.log4j.*" />
    <fileset dir="${classes.dir}/demo">
      <exclude name="*Test.class" />
    </fileset>
  </cobertura-instrument>
</target>
```

Note the following things about this target. First, the file set can include more than just Java classes; JAR and WAR archives are valid and will

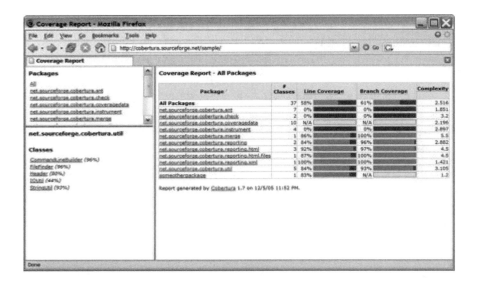

Figure 10.1: Cobertura package-level coverage report

be instrumented accordingly. Next, there are two options for specifying and filtering classes to be instrumented. You can specify a regular expression in the ignore tag that will exclude files, or you can use the include and exclude tags in the fileset tag.

At this point, manual or automated testing can proceed. If you are using automated testing, be sure to place the instrumented classes (produced by the previous step) in the classpath before other classes. If you don't, no results or incorrect percentages will be produced.

Once the testing has been completed, the final step is to generate a report from the results. This can take many forms, from XML or HTML, to PDF or Swing applications. The following Ant code will create XML and HTML reports in Cobertura:

```
<target name="coverage-report" >
  <cobertura-report srcdir="${src.dir}"
                    destdir="${coverage.xml.dir}" format="xml" />
  <cobertura-report srcdir="${src.dir}"
                    destdir="${coverage.html.dir}" />
</target>
```

In the resulting code coverage report, you can drill down into packages and classes. At each of these levels, you will see two percentages:

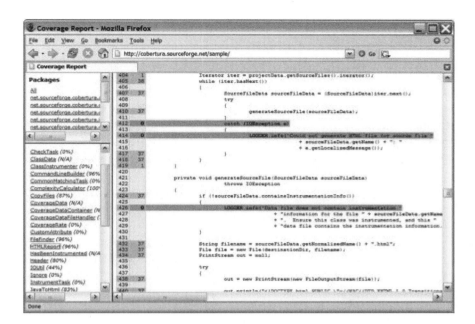

Figure 10.2: COBERTURA CLASS-LEVEL COVERAGE REPORT

- *Line coverage.* This is the percentage of the lines of code that were executed. For each line of code in the application, you can determine whether it was executed.

- *Branch coverage.* This is the percentage of conditional code executed. This expands upon the previous number. For complete coverage, every logical condition in every branching statement needs to have been exercised.

Figure 10.1 shows an example of the Cobertura package-level report. The Cobertura class-level report appears in Figure 10.2.

Depending on the tool, there may be more information. Cobertura provides two additional metrics, McCabe's Cyclomatic Complexity[2] for all methods, and the number of times the line of code was executed at the class level.

McCabe's Cyclomatic Complexity

---

[2]This is a great metric to have. Basically, the more complex the methods, the more likely bugs will be hiding in them. You will get a better return on effort by adding tests to increase the code coverage percentages in these methods and classes. You can find a complete definition of the metric at http://en.wikipedia.org/wiki/Cyclomatic_complexity.

10.2 Zeroing In on Hard-to-Test Code

The first technique we will look at to improve testing effectiveness is using code coverage when first creating the tests.

When you are working with existing code, you never have a guarantee that unit tests have been developed. Reasons for not having tests range from the code being developed before agile techniques were common to highly coupled classes where the time and risk to split the classes and write the tests doesn't exist in the project timeline.

Whatever the case, the time has now come to write unit tests as a safety net for those who come after you. If you are retroactively writing testing code, you may not have the time to test the entire class, so you need to focus on the more complex and high-risk sections of the class. This scenario is more often the case in legacy code that is highly coupled or code that has complex or uncommon logic and algorithms.

The steps are intuitive, and by iteratively repeating them, you can obtain the desired level of code coverage:

1. *Remove any existing data files or databases.* It is important to ensure that the data being generated is correct for the current iteration. Always remember to remove old data so that the results will be correct for the current test run.

2. *Review the code coverage results from the last iteration.* Take a look at the report to see whether the lines of code being targeted were executed, and whether all the necessary branch conditions and adverse or error conditions were covered. If this is the first iteration, you can skip this step.

3. *Update the unit tests that exercise the code you are targeting.* You have covered all the code and conditions in step 2 that you are targeting, you are done. Otherwise, update the unit tests to incorporate those conditions that were previously missed.

4. *Run the tests against code that has been instrumented.* The final step is to run the new unit test code against the instrumented application code.

The key point to remember is that you are after a *desired* level of coverage. The more complex the code (and the relationships) and the closer you get to 100% coverage, the more time it will take to develop the tests

Where Did 85% Come From?

I'm not sure anyone really knows why this number seems to be the standard percentage quoted, but I tend to agree with Brian Marick in his article "How to Misuse Code Coverage."* He suggests that 85% has been passed from person to person and from organization to organization, and that if followed back far enough, you would most likely find that this number was "pulled out of a hat."

To determine the correct percentage for your application, you need to determine the code coverage percentage at which any further increase involves a significant increase in the amount of testing code.

In general, a percentage from 80–90% seems to be the widely accepted norm. This is substantiated by Brian Marick as well as others, including Howard Lewis Ship[†] and Robert Grady in his book *Practical Software Metrics for Project Management and Process Improvement*.

*http://www.testing.com/writings/coverage.pdf
[†]http://howardlewisship.com/blog/2005/09/code-coverage-metrics-and-testing.html

to keep the code coverage percentage increasing. This follows the law of diminishing returns.[3]

law of diminishing returns

The generally accepted percentage at which returns start diminishing for code coverage is 85%—whether you can achieve higher or lower than this number depends on the code you are working with and the time in the project plan allotted per feature (which should include the developer testing). My suggestion is to try a few iterations to see whether you can meet the desired percentage. If it cannot be met, decide on a percentage with your project manager or project sponsor that balances the time required to write the tests with the coverage obtained. Also, remember that the percentages do not need to be the same for the entire project and can be adjusted at a package level.

[3]http://www.answers.com/topic/law-of-diminishing-returns

10.3 Maintain Code Coverage Percentages Over the Life of the Project

Now that you have decided upon levels of code coverage on a package or project level and have developed tests that adhere to that level, you want to ensure that the percentages are maintained during the introduction of new code and during modifications to existing code. The way to ensure this is to instrument the application code, run the automated developer tests, and generate code coverage reports during the build process. The reports then need to be reviewed to ensure the code coverage percentages have been met.

The Cobertura-specific Ant tasks that instrument the code and generate reports have already been discussed, but an additional task allows the build to automatically fail if prescribed percentages are not met:

```
<cobertura-check haltonfailure="true" branchrate="80" linerate="80">
  <regex pattern="example.gui.*" branchrate="85" linerate="90"/>
  <regex pattern="example.model.*" branchrate="55" linerate="80"/>
  <regex pattern="example.services.*" branchrate="85" linerate="95"/>
</cobertura-check>
```

The pattern matching for packages includes attributes for only branch rate and line rate, but there is a full range of options for the parent <cobertura-check> tag. For each attribute the value is from 0 to 100, and the options available are shown in Figure 10.3, on the facing page.

When using this technique, it is vitally important to understand why the percentage values were selected and the context in which the numbers will be used. Peer reviewing the developer tests, having formal written policies around writing the tests (such as, "simple getters and setters do not need to be tested"), and knowing how the code review percentages were selected will help. It is also a good idea to review the code coverage percentages on a weekly basis, recording any significant changes in a project log (following the same example from earlier—you might record "the total project percentages dropped 10% this week because we added a number of new model objects"). There is nothing worse than a project manager, who is looking only at the percentages over time and out of context, approaching you at the end of development and inquiring why quality has dropped.

Attribute	Description
branchrate	The minimum acceptable branch coverage rate needed by each class
linerate	The minimum acceptable line coverage rate needed by each class
packagebranchrate	The minimum acceptable average branch coverage rate needed by each package
packagelinerate	The minimum acceptable average line coverage rate needed by each package
totalbranchrate	The minimum acceptable average branch coverage rate needed by the project as a whole
totallinerate	The minimum acceptable average line coverage rate needed by the project as a whole

Figure 10.3: COBERTURA OPTIONS

10.4   Comparing User and Developer Testing Percentages

The last technique for improving testing effectiveness is to compare the code coverage percentages when a user is exercising the application (or automated tests mimicking this behavior) to the percentages from running the developer tests.

The benefit of this approach is that it gives you a realistic baseline of what code the users are actually exercising when running the application and, thus, what developer testing should cover.

In fact, because the developer testing should exercise the less common logic flows and exception cases, it should always have higher code coverage percentages.

Here are the steps:

1. *Instrument the code and deploy the application.* You could instrument the application during the build process, but I think in this case it is a better option to instrument the final file that is going to be deployed. This way, the name can be changed (to something like myproject_instr.war) to avoid accidentally having the file go into production.

2. *Run user tests through the application, and collect the code coverage results.* Before starting, make sure that the code coverage database has been removed. Once removed, the testing can proceed. If your organization has automated tests, they can be run. Otherwise, someone manually running all the test scripts will do just as well. When complete, you want to generate code coverage reports from the collected data. Remember to move the generated reports to a different location for safekeeping.

3. *Run the automated developer tests, and collect the code coverage results.* Once again, make sure the code coverage database has been removed. Run the automated tests on the application, and generate the code coverage report. If you have the resources, run the automated developer testing and the user testing concurrently on different machines—just make sure that the application code is the same.

4. *Compare the results.* This is the most manual step, because Cobertura doesn't provide any tools to compare two sets of coverage data. Rather than going down to the class level, focus on the line coverage and branch coverage at the package level. Because the first page of the HTML report provides the percentages for each individual package as well as the total for all packages, it is a simple task to compare them.

Once you have generated and compared the results, you can achieve and surpass concrete code coverage percentage goals—not only at a project level but at a package and class level as well. This is important. A common practice to improve code coverage from a developer test perspective (usually when deadlines are tight) is to add testing coverage to methods that are easy to test but do not provide any additional quality benefit (providing test cases for simple getters and setters is again a good example). It will be easy to determine whether quality is improving in the necessary places if these classes are isolated in the same package.

10.5   Conclusion

The three techniques covered in this chapter will help improve testing effectiveness, allowing you to productively pinpoint where more test coverage is needed and enabling you to maintain the code coverage results throughout the life of the project. The key point to remember is that you cannot leave code coverage analysis until the last minute—it needs to be an integral part of your development process. This way, you can craft tests that better target problematic code and quickly react to trends in the quality of your software. Knowing sooner, rather than later, is the only way to find time in the project plan to address quality issues and proactively address the question of code quality before it is asked.

Chapter 11

Extreme Decorator: Total Object Makeover

by Brian Sletten

Brian Sletten is a liberal arts–educated software engineer focusing on forward-leaning technologies. He has a background as a system architect, a developer, a mentor, and a trainer. His experience spans defense, finance, and commercial domains, with security consulting and software development involving network matrix switches, 3D simulation/visualization, Grid Computing, P2P, and Semantic web-based systems. He has a bachelor's degree in computer science from the College of William and Mary and currently lives in Fairfax, Virginia, where he and his wife run Bosatsu Consulting, Inc.

Brian's recent favorite books and technical discoveries are listed starting on page 219.

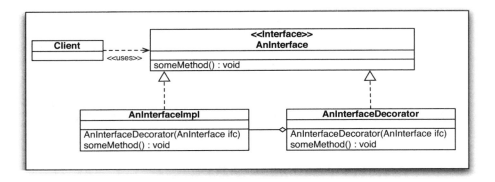

Figure 11.1: DECORATOR PATTERN

A few years ago television programs about decorating someone else's house, apartment, or car became all the rage. The owner started with something basic, and somebody else came in and improved upon it by adding their own style or extra features. The results were often not what the original owner anticipated, but they usually liked them. The shows made for good television, and still seem popular today.

Decorator pattern The Decorator pattern works in much the same way, although it is unlikely to result in quite as compelling television. The intent of this pattern is to allow an object to be wrapped at run-time to compose it with extra behavior, often in ways unanticipated by the class designer. The original object is held by the decorating instance which delegates to the inner target when and if it sees fit. An example of the structural relationship between the participants appears in Figure 11.1.

The mechanism works because the client knows about the object in question only through the interface by which it is held. The decorating instance also implements this interface but does something the orig- *separation of concerns* inal class did not do. This is an example of separation of concerns, a goal of computer scientists for the last 30 years that has motivated the adoption of structured, object-oriented, and now aspect-oriented programming. By allowing a class consumer to pick and choose what behavior she wants dynamically, the same code can cleanly respond to different circumstances in a wide variety of ways.

Many developers do not realize that they've probably been using the Decorator pattern for as long as they've been using Java. The basic byte-oriented I/O streams from the java.io package are a canonical example of Decorator in action. Perhaps you've wondered why you need an InputStream to create a BufferedInputStream. It's because Buffered-InputStream simply adds buffering capabilities to the underlying byte-oriented features. It needs a source from which to consume data, though, so we need to provide it in the constructor. The following code demonstrates the basic usage of buffering data from a compressed file:

```
InputStream is = new FileInputStream( "myfile.gz" );
is = new GZIPInputStream( is );
is = new BufferedInputStream( is );
```

You may argue that buffering is a common enough I/O task that Sun should have just added it to the basic InputStream class. The problem is that you may not always want or need buffering features, or they may not be supported by your underlying transport. You may also want to buffer at a different layer. The point is that the consumer of the InputStream class knows better than Sun engineers when and where she needs buffering. As such, it is great that they allowed her to make that decision. Even if you did successfully lobby to get buffering added to the InputStream class, what then? Filtering? Zip compression? GZip compression? Any number of capabilities might be desirable only some of the time. Encumbering the basic I/O capability with all of these features would penalize developers who did not need them and make the APIs harder to learn.

In general, the Sun engineers made a good choice in separating the concerns of byte-oriented I/O, buffering, compression, and so on. I will explain in the *Consequences* section why I will concede only that they made a good choice "in general."

Given that developers are familiar with the I/O wrapper implementations provided by the JDK libraries, it seems strange they do not think about creating their own extensions more often. I'm going to show that there are several ways in which decorating InputStream instances with your own custom implementation of the Decorator pattern can provide easy and useful ways to manipulate the stream.

To move beyond the standard Decorator pattern I/O classes, we will create a few somewhat realistic scenarios. We will, of course, leave out many nitty-gritty details, but you will propably find a good starting point for extending our examples.

11.1 Scenario 1

A company, Value Products, Inc., takes payment information from its customers in its retail stores. These records get aggregated for the day and submitted to a central billing system to process the charges. The file format as follows (note these are not real credit card numbers, so please do not attempt to use them!):

```
Customer Account Activity
Date:      1/10/2006
Store:     #1678
Account              Payment Method          Amount
123458               3425987987987324        $123.12
134580               4720987987988233        $215.82
158222               2426687980012345        $99.79
164358               6743079879873241        $520.57
177758               4748250079798732        $110.33
195800               5525017987986339        $49.99
```

Historically, these files were then sent by FTP to a report generator server that would summarize the purchases for its customers on a monthly basis. Being a hip, trendy company, Value Products is moving to a service-oriented architecture and now wants to POST an XML version of the report to a RESTful service. A schema is generated for the request; it looks like the example in this listing:

service-oriented architecture

```
<REPORTSUMMARY>
  <STORE>1234</STORE>
  <REPORT>
    <![CDATA[
      <!-- REPORT GOES HERE -->
    ]]>
  </REPORT>
</REPORTSUMMARY>
```

JDOM

When discussing how to do this, one developer suggests creating a JDOM document, reading the file into a string and adding a CDATA section to the <REPORT> element. Although this will certainly work for small reports and low volumes of data, it is unnecessarily memory-intensive; we do not need to commit the entire report to memory. If we are just going to be POSTing the file to a RESTful service, we can be clever and use the Decorator pattern to wrap the underlying FileInput-Stream.

The first realization that assists us is that we want the data consumer to read from a series of independent streams in succession. The first one will serve up the first part of the wrapper schema. Once it is done with the initial part of the wrapper, it needs to read from the wrapped InputStream itself. When all the original data has been read, it needs to consume the last part of the schema. The JDK helper class SequenceInputStream provides just this behavior. It takes either an Enumeration<InputStream> or two InputStreams.

Although we could certainly just use a SequenceInputStream directly to solve our problem, we would be exposing implementation details in a way we would rather not do. These details would also be scattered to every use of our report-wrapping feature. Instead, we will create a class called ReportInputStream that takes in a String source name and an InputStream. Presumably, the source identifies the store and is extracted from a filename or directory in which the report file is found. Our goal is to use the ReportInputStream as we do in this listing:

```java
InputStream is = new FileInputStream(dataFile);
is = new ReportInputStream("1678", is);

byte [] buffer = new byte[2048];
ByteArrayOutputStream baos = new ByteArrayOutputStream();
int numRead = 0;

while ((numRead = is.read(buffer))  >= 0) {
  if (numRead > 0) {
    baos.write(buffer, 0, numRead);
  }
}
```

All the implementation details are contained within the class that is shown in the following listing. The Enumeration passed to the SequenceInputStream constructor is satisfied by an inner class that maintains a list of InputStreams; one for the schema header, one for the report body, and one for the schema footer. Each is consumed in turn by the mechanics of the parent SequenceInputStream.

`code/Decorator/net/bosatsu/util/report/ReportInputStream.java`

```java
package net.bosatsu.util.report;
import java.io.ByteArrayInputStream;
import java.io.InputStream;
import java.io.SequenceInputStream;
import java.util.ArrayList;
import java.util.Enumeration;
import java.util.List;

/**
 * Modularize wrapping a particular InputStream with XML elements by
 * defining three separate InputStreams and serving them up to the
 * parent SequenceInputStream.
```

```
 *
 * Demonstrate one potential custom Decorator pattern implementation.
 * @author bsletten
 */

public class ReportInputStream extends SequenceInputStream
{
    /*
     * Constructor that takes some arbitrary String source identifier
     * and the underlying InputStream to wrap.
     */
    public ReportInputStream( String source, InputStream is ) {
        super( new StreamEnumerator( source, is ) );
    }

    /**
     * The inner class simply maintains the list of InputStreams for the
     * parent SequenceInputStream to iterate over.
     *
     * @author bsletten
     */
    public static class StreamEnumerator implements Enumeration <InputStream> {
        private List <InputStream> streamList = new ArrayList <InputStream>();

        public StreamEnumerator( String source, InputStream is ) {
            // We want to wrap the underlying input stream with XML
            // elements satisfying some schema perhaps for submitting
            // to a RESTful web service. A different set of values
            // could wrap the InputStream with a SOAP request. In
            // addition to decorating existing data sources into these
            // request forms transparently, by relying on the stream
            // interfaces, we can avoid having to read the entire data
            // source into memory all at once.

            streamList.add( new ByteArrayInputStream(
                new String( "<REPORTSUMMARY><STORE>" + source +
                "</STORE><REPORT><![CDATA[\n" ).getBytes() ) );
            streamList.add( is );
            streamList.add( new ByteArrayInputStream(
                new String( "\n]]></REPORT></REPORTSUMMARY>" ).getBytes() ) );
        }

        public boolean hasMoreElements() {
            return streamList.size() > 0;
        }

        public InputStream nextElement() {
            return streamList.remove( 0 );
        }
    }
}
```

We separated the stream-wrapping concern into a RESTful request and so were able to satisfy the requirements without tangling the submission code with too many irrelevant details. This way, if we need to wrap the report into a SOAP request, we could just choose a different instance of the Decorator pattern to provide that functionality.

Because the Decorator pattern works on instances of classes that satisfy an interface, it is necessary to be able to intercept the object creation or hand-code the wrapping as we did in the previous listing. Java does not have the ability to intercept object creation like C++, Ruby, and Objective-C do, so we might want to request an instance of the InputStream from a factory instance, as shown in this listing:

```
InputStream is = InputStreamFactory.getInputStream(dataFile);
// Now we can use the InputStream unaware of the actual composition
```

The factory might respond to the name of the file, where it was found, or some other system property to decide how to wrap the created instance. The point is that the InputStream client would not need to know or care about the particulars of the source of the data, or what was happening to it along the way. It simply knows it is consuming data from a stream.

Applying the ReportInputStream to our sample data file results in output that looks like this:

```
<REPORTSUMMARY>
  <STORE>1678</STORE>
  <REPORT>
    <![CDATA[
  Customer Account Activity
  Date:   1/10/2006
  Store:  #1678
  Account         Payment Method          Amount
  -------         --------------          -------
  123458          3425987987987324        $123.12
  134580          4720987987988233        $215.82
  158222          2426687980012345        $99.79
  164358          6743079879873241        $520.57
  177758          4748250079798732        $110.33
  195800          5525017987986339        $49.99
    ]]>
  </REPORT>
</REPORTSUMMARY>
```

A pleasant side effect of this approach is that we can wrap any InputStream with our ReportInputStream, not just FileInputStream instances. We could extract the stream from any open URL, such as for a website or other REST-based service, and pass that into our new code.

11.2 Scenario 2

After our system in Scenario 1 is tested and released, Value Products decides it wants to undertake an effort to protect its customers' credit card data to avoid any embarrassing incidents and to satisfy the external audits it knows are coming. Management decides that this initiative is the new high priority (not at the expense of all the other high priorities, though). Each team is responsible for protecting their part of the enterprise system.

The files are submitted to the accounting servers in an encrypted form, so they are protected until they are handed off to be processed for reporting. The data stored in the accounting databases requires special handling to maintain the full credit card in a protected form in case accounting needs to recharge or adjust the amount in the future. The reporting system, however, has no further need of the actual credit card information before returning it to customers. It would be useful to show the customers the last four digits of the card that was used, so we want to maintain at least that much of the number.

The reporting service team meets to discuss the effort required to mask the credit cards in all the reports (including several formats other than what we are discussing in this chapter). Some well-intentioned engineer gets up and draws some diagrams on the whiteboard describing how he wants to put a new process in place. Files will be dropped into a directory where they will be lexically parsed based on the document format (he can barely contain his glee at the prospect of whipping out his old-school Unix fu). Once the report is parsed, the masking of the relevant data can occur, and the file can be rewritten out before moving it back to where it would be picked up by the existing report submission system.

After some discussion about keeping the number of moving parts of the system to a minimum, another engineer points out that they are already converting the files using the ReportInputStream code. It seems like it would be possible to work within that code to mask the credit cards. Someone else points out that it would be a good idea to keep the masking code separate from the existing report-wrapping code. A new use of the Decorator pattern could isolate this new feature.

The team decides that there probably is no actual need to parse the data with something like lex because credit cards have a definite form, easily distinguished from most surrounding text. Particularly in the current set of files there should be no identifiers or data values that look like credit cards but are not. It seems like matching credit cards with a regular expression will solve the company's parsing needs in the short term. If it needs to put in some other constraints to avoid transforming data that does not represent a credit card, the company can add them later.

After performing this analysis, the team decides to solve the problem with a RegularExpressionInputStream capable of doing transformations of data identified by arbitrary regular expressions. Although they are only focusing on credit card data now, they think a general-purpose tool would be useful because other forms of data might need to be transformed in the future. The full code to implement this is too complicated to list fully here, but we will show some relevant parts. Its use would be similar to what we have seen before. This is shown in this listing:

```
InputStream is = new FileInputStream(dataFile);
RegularExpressionReplacer rer = new RegularExpressionReplacer();
rer.addPatternMapping( Pattern.compile( "\\b(\\d{16})\\b" ),
                       new CCMaskRegularExpressionTransformer() );
is = new RegularExpressionInputStream(is, rer);
is = new ReportInputStream("1678", is);
```

This example shows wrapping the FileInputStream with a RegularExpressionInputStream before using our earlier ReportInputStream. The RegularExpressionReplacer class maps the specified patterns to functional transformers, in this case a CCMaskRegularExpressionTransformer instance. The RegularExpressionInputStream converts the underlying InputStream into a series of lines using a BufferedReader. This will work only on text-oriented data streams, but that should not be a big concession to make. The read method looks like this:

```
public int read() throws IOException {
  int retValue = EOF;

  // If we have a buffer
  if( buffer != null ) {
    // And it isn't empty
    if( bufferIndex &lt; buffer.length ) {
      // Read the next byte
      retValue = buffer[ bufferIndex++ ];
    } else {
      // We have hit the end of our line. Grab the next line
      // and transform anything that matches any of our patterns.
      fetchAndTransformNextLine();

      // We need to indicate the EOL
```

```
        retValue = EOL;
      }
    }
    return retValue;
  }

  private void fetchAndTransformNextLine() throws IOException {
    String line = br.readLine();

    bufferIndex = 0;

    if( line != null ) {
      buffer = rer.performTransformations( line ).getBytes();
    } else {
      buffer = null;
    }
  }
```

fetchAndTransformNextLine() reads the next line from BufferedReader and passes it to RegularExpressionReplacer to transform any patterns that are matched. This transformed line is held in the buffer from which we get our bytes. As we hit the end of the buffer, we repeat the process and consume and transform the next line. Within the RegularExpression-Replacer instance, each Transformer object's transform() method is called when its associated pattern is matched. Here we use a CCMaskRegular-ExpressionTransformer, which is shown in the following listing:

code/Decorator/net/bosatsu/util/regex/cc/CCMaskRegularExpressionTransformer.java

```
package net.bosatsu.util.regex.cc;

import java.util.regex.Matcher;

import net.bosatsu.util.regex.io.Transformer;

/**
 * A concrete implementation of the Transformer interface that simply masks
 * a 16-digit credit card by concatenating the last four digits to a bunch
 * of Xs. A real implementation of this would need to guarantee the validity
 * of the credit card (rather than simply matching digits) and to support
 * different credit card lengths.
 *
 * @author bsletten
 */
public class CCMaskRegularExpressionTransformer implements Transformer {
    public String transform(Matcher m) {
        String retValue = "XXXXXXXXXXXX" + m.group().substring( 12 );
        return retValue;
    }
}
```

Executing this code on our reports results in something like this:

```
<REPORTSUMMARY>
  <STORE>1678</STORE>
  <REPORT>
    <![CDATA[
  Customer Account Activity
  Date:   1/10/2006
  Store:  #1678
  Account         Payment Method         Amount
  -------         ----------------       -------
  123458          XXXXXXXXXXXX7324       $123.12
  134580          XXXXXXXXXXXX8233       $215.82
  158222          XXXXXXXXXXXX2345       $99.79
  164358          XXXXXXXXXXXX3241       $520.57
  177758          XXXXXXXXXXXX8732       $110.33
  195800          XXXXXXXXXXXX6339       $49.99
    ]]>
  </REPORT>
</REPORTSUMMARY>
```

The real issues of providing real credit card protection against arbitrary data file formats are much more complicated. It would be straightforward, however, to add support for managing different credit card lengths, the existence of non-credit-card data that matches our regular expressions, and so on, into our CCMaskRegularExpressionTransformer class. The goal here is simply to show the composition of behavior using the Decorator pattern.

11.3 Scenario 3

Based largely on its success in keeping customer data safe and writing clever software to manage costs, Value Products' stock price rises over time. Feeling flush with value (it is not just a clever name, after all), the company goes on a purchasing binge and acquires some of its competitors. Although it is simple enough to install its point-of-sale systems in the newly acquired retail locations, there is the issue of mapping the parent company's customer account information into the subsidiary company's databases before issuing purchase activity reports. The company sets up an account service that is capable of doing the lookup, but we still need to apply the account transformation before the reporting system.

The team gets together to discuss this new requirement and realizes that they have already laid the groundwork for what needs to be done. The files that show up can be identified by whether they are from an original or newly acquired store. The reports from the latter category can be transformed using another Transformer class that calls into the AccountService to make the transformation. The following listing shows the extra code being added to support this behavior:

```
InputStream is = new FileInputStream(dataFile);
RegularExpressionReplacer rer = new RegularExpressionReplacer();
rer.addPatternMapping( Pattern.compile( "\\b(\\d{16})\\b" ),
                       new CCMaskRegularExpressionTransformer() );
rer.addPatternMapping( Pattern.compile( "^(\\d{6})\\b" ),
                       new AccountRegularExpressionTransformer() );
is = new RegularExpressionInputStream(is, rer);
is = new ReportInputStream("1678", is);
```

In this case, any six-digit number matched at the start of the line is considered an account number and is transformed by the AccountRegularExpressionTransformer class, which can be seen in this listing:

code/Decorator/net/bosatsu/util/regex/account/AccountRegularExpressionTransformer.java

```
package net.bosatsu.util.regex.account;

import java.util.regex.Matcher;
import net.bosatsu.util.regex.io.Transformer;

/**
 * A concrete implementation of the Transformer interface
 * that transforms an account ID selected via a regular expression
 * by looking up a different account ID from some service.
 *
 * @author bsletten
 */

public class AccountRegularExpressionTransformer implements Transformer
{
    public String transform(Matcher m) {
        String oldAccount = m.group();
        return AccountService.getNewAccount( oldAccount );
    }
}
```

The final output appears in the following listing. The good news is that once the customer account databases get synced up, we can easily extract this code without affecting anything else. In fact, it might be a good idea to interrogate a property to see whether we need it. That way, it can be shut off without a code change.

```
<REPORTSUMMARY>
  <STORE>1678</STORE>
    <REPORT>
      <![CDATA[
```

```
Customer Account Activity
Date:   1/10/2006
Store:  #1678
Account          Payment Method        Amount
-------          ----------------      -------
01234-123458     XXXXXXXXXXXX7324      $123.12
01234-134580     XXXXXXXXXXXX8233      $215.82
01234-158222     XXXXXXXXXXXX2345      $99.79
01234-164358     XXXXXXXXXXXX3241      $520.57
01234-177758     XXXXXXXXXXXX8732      $110.33
01234-195800     XXXXXXXXXXXX6339      $49.99
     ]]>
  </REPORT>
</REPORTSUMMARY>
```

After running the new code, the team realizes they will need to compensate in the event that RegularExpressionInputStream changes the length of what it transforms by adding or removing characters. In the previous listing, this might involve eating spaces after the transformed accounts. These and other details are left as an exercise for the reader.

11.4 Consequences

Although I have clearly glossed over many of the details in these contrived scenarios, I hope I have demonstrated how the Decorator pattern can be used to modularize particular concerns so that they may be composed dynamically as necessary. This keeps us from tangling implementation details that are unrelated. It also allows us to make the choice of what gets called in response to run-time context. In our scenarios, reports from different stores might require the AccountRegularExpressionTransformer or not. It would be great to hide that fact from the code that was reading in the data to keep it simple and focused on what it is doing.

A consequence of the elegance of the JDK I/O design is that it requires a least-common-denominator approach to traversing the streams; in this case, it is the byte-oriented nature that facilitates the various higher-level abstractions. The problem is that for large data sets, this approach does not perform well. Even the use of buffering wrappers does not help when you are talking about gigabytes or terabytes of data. For this reason, in JDK 1.4 Sun introduced NIO, the new I/O capabilities. These forgo this design approach. Instead, they focus specifically on mechanisms that promote performance for big data sets.

Java I/O streams are not the only application of the Decorator pattern. Other examples include caching, synchronization, logging, and other concerns that you might require for your objects in some circumstances but not others.

There are consequences and complications to this pattern, though. First, the Decorator pattern requires the use of interfaces and wrapping instances. If you do not have a relevant interface or did not plan for wrapping the instances, it can be difficult or impossible to adopt the Decorator pattern in your system. If the code that you are trying to put into a Decorator implementation fundamentally changes class invariants of the decorated instance, perhaps this is not an appropriate approach either.

aspect-oriented programming

Second, the Decorator pattern also requires you to provide implementations of all of the methods in an interface even if you want to decorate only a few. It certainly is possible have "empty" methods that simply delegate to the inner instance, but too much of that starts to feel like a waste of time. Additionally, it is possible to decorate only instances and not, say, classes or collections of classes. If you find yourself needing to do these more advanced kinds of decoration, you may want to look at aspect-oriented programming as a more general way to modularize concerns.

11.5 Conclusion

Although innovative Decorator patterns may never make compelling prime-time television, they may allow you to quickly respond to new requirements in simple and elegant ways. By allowing developers to deal with different execution scenarios and customer needs by composing behavior at run-time, it is possible to take a basic object and give it a total makeover, turning it into exactly what is needed in a given situation.

Chapter 12

From Fragility to Agility: Methodologies and Practices

by Venkat Subramaniam

Dr. Venkat Subramaniam, founder of Agile Developer, Inc., has trained and mentored more than 3,000 software developers in the United States, Canada, and Europe. Venkat helps his clients effectively apply and succeed with agile practices on their software projects. He speaks frequently at conferences. Venkat is also an adjunct professor for the practice of computer science at University of Houston and teaches at Rice University School for Continuing Studies. He is the author of .NET Gotchas [Sub05] and coauthor of Practices of an Agile Developer [Sub06].

Software development has come to be a fragile endeavor. According to one study,[1] less than 10% of software development projects succeed. Would we tolerate such an abysmal rate of success in any other field of work? How can we turn our development efforts into success stories? We will address that question in this chapter. We'll first talk about agility, then we'll discuss some of the agile methodologies.

What (and Why) Is Agility?

Agility is defined, in the Merriam-Webster dictionary, as "marked by ready ability to move with quick easy grace." Agility is having a quick, resourceful, and adaptable character. Being agile is really not as much a technical matter as it is a matter of your attitude.

Let's start with an everyday example. A driver on a busy highway switches on the turn signal to move into the adjacent lane. What happens next in most major cities? Sadly, the person behind our driver but one lane over lane speeds up, blocking the way and leaving our driver frustrated. Next time, our clever driver decides to jump lanes without signaling. This may provoke a response from the driver behind, often a wave with fewer than five fingers. Some of these situations escalate to road rage. The same two people walking toward a door generally act in a civilized way, but put them behind a wheel and....

Imagine, again, our driver turns on his signal. The person in the next lane eases the accelerator, signaling our driver to go ahead with the lane change. Our ever-polite driver waves back happily, thanking the neighbor—same situation, different attitude, different result.

Navigating through your project is like navigating ever-changing traffic patterns. It requires agility and attitude. If our attitude is to resist change or if our planning makes it harder to make changes, then we're setting ourselves up for failure.

But, you say, experts have given us some rigorous methodologies in the past. Can't we succeed using them? Unfortunately, the answer is no. Although some of these rigorous methodologies were introduced with good intent, they have failed to yield results.

---

[1]Capers Jones, "Software Project Management Practices: Failure versus Success," http://www.stsc.hill.af.mil/crosstalk/2004/10/0410Jones.html

Until the early 19th century, the death rate after surgery was very high; those who survived surgery were likely to die from infection. The experts of that time did not figure out that unsanitary conditions were causing infection. Some doctors actually carried the infection to patients. Joseph Lister's germ theory and antiseptic procedures, which are established standards today, were received with doubt, indifference, and hostility. It takes time for us—humans—to figure out what works.

Most of the methodologies proposed in the past decades have tried to make software development an engineering activity. Folks reasoned that engineers are successful, so if we do what they're doing, we should succeed as well. Software development is still a nascent field, and it is not entirely engineering.[2] There is a lot of learning to do, and it is important to keep our minds open to ideas that will help us succeed. Simply borrowing ideas and practices from other fields may not help. History has taught us that merely attaching wings to a machine does not make an airplane.

12.1 Key to Agile Development

What makes software development different (and special)? If you ask me how much time and money I'd need to manufacture 10,000 cell phones, I can give you a fairly decent and reliable estimate. However, can you guess how much time it took to commercialize the first cell phone? Thirty-seven years![3] It takes a heck a lot of effort and time to create something new. Craig Larman's *Agile and Iterative Development: A Manager's Guide* [Lar04] states that software development is an innovative process—not predictive manufacturing.

In any nontrivial development project, the users gain a better understanding of what they need as they get to see what is being developed. Some of the things they thought of as important turn out not to be important. Other things, often conceived of only later, suddenly become urgent.

Software developers are often unfamiliar with the domain of the application being developed. This makes it harder to communicate, because communication is easier when people share a context. It takes fewer

---

[2]Alistair Cockburn, "The End of Software Engineering and the Start of Economic-Cooperative Gaming,"
http://alistair.cockburn.us/crystal/articles/eoseatsoecg/theendofsoftwareengineering.htm.
[3]http://inventors.about.com/library/weekly/aa070899.htm

words to express yourself when you're in sync—at times, all it takes is a look or a smile, as in social settings. Assume I have little understanding of atomic physics. How do I, as a strong software developer, help design and implement a control system for a nuclear reactor? Dropping a 100-page (or 1,000-page) document on my desk is not much help. I could read it and still develop a perfectly functional reactor that blows up.

Documents are often misinterpreted. Generally, the longer the document is, the less I grasp all that is being said. The document may have expressed one expert's view but may not be agreed upon by all the stakeholders on the project.

How do we then make sure we actually deliver what the customers want, especially when the customers themselves may not fully know what they want? Communication is the key.

Imagine that I take some requirements then go off to design and implement them. Within a week or two, I get the customers together and show them what I've done. I ask them them to play with it and solicit their feedback. What will they do? They'll tell me whether I have met their requirements and how I should proceed further, including what changes, if any, I need to make. If I am totally off, I find out in a week or two from the time they give me the spec, not months later—a week before we go into production.

I'm not suggesting that documents are unnecessary. I am suggesting that we can't rely solely on documents if we want to understand requirements. Interaction and collaboration are critical to the success of our projects.

We take their input, get the work done quickly and in small steps, show them what we've done, and ask them to steer us further, and then we move forward based on what they really want. That's what agility in development is all about.

12.2 The Hypocrisy of Timelines

In January, your team starts work on a project with a predefined deadline of November 1st. On September 1st, you realize that things may not be going well. You approach the boss, who is busy browsing the Web, with the question "Is the deadline in 60 days firm?" You got his attention. He looks at you for a minute, takes a deep breath, and says, "Yes, we better be done by then. Any questions?" You walk away determined to do your best. Your team works a lot of late nights and weekends. Finally, you throw a binary over the fence on or around November 1st. Then what happens? It is not unheard of that companies spend the next weeks to several months fixing bugs. If, after three months, you're still fixing bugs, did you really get the project done on time? As an industry, we have been kidding ourselves for too long with deadlines, estimations, and planning. As an industry, we're hypocritical about timelines.

If project managers and nontechnical people decide the timeline and they do so upfront when they have the least understanding of the project, how realistic are these estimates?

Three factors influence our progress: scope, time, and quality. Like the old Triangle maxim (fast, cheap, or good), you let your customers and management pick two of these three influences. If they set the timeline and a certain amount of quality is important, then you get to negotiate the scope. If scope and time are critical (as they are with a business trying to be first in the market with a proof of concept), then you may have to compromise on the quality to get ahead, provided that is clearly understood by all involved. What if your customers and/or management insist that they get to pick all three—scope, time, and quality? Then they get to enjoy the fourth factor—failure.

If two factors are picked for you, how do you estimate and measure your progress on the third factor? Iterative and incremental development can help. Start the ten-month project, but within three weeks demo what you have done so far, and let your customers exercise your code and evaluate the progress. Repeat this every three weeks.[4] Don't wait until the end to find out that your project is doomed. Take the pulse of the progress every few weeks, and steer the development based on current conditions—reassessing and reprioritizing appropriately. Everyone involved in the project development—managers, customers, and developers—participates in the success of the project (and decides how to define that success).

---

[4]Refer to "Feel the Rhythm" in *Practices of an Agile Developer* [Sub06]

12.3 Agile Methodologies

Software methodology is what we do to create software. It's a series of related methods to coordinate our team's activities. We seek guidance from methodologies (and methodologists) to learn how to get our work done, to understand our responsibilities and priorities, and to help us measure and show progress. A methodology can serve as a framework for learning and practicing development skills.

A number of lightweight methodologies have been introduced by people interested in improving the reputation of software development. In this section, we'll take a look at the key features of these methodologies.

eXtreme Programming (XP)

Kent Beck, Ward Cunningham, and Ron Jeffries (and others) introduced XP in *eXtreme Programming Explained* [Bec00] based on their experience on the C3 project. XP is based on four values and twelve principles.

Features

The four values of XP are communication, simplicity, feedback, and courage. As we discussed earlier, communication is critical to make sure we're converging toward stability and meeting the expectations of customers. By keeping things simple, we avoid unnecessary complexity, and we keep the code understandable and maintainable. Keeping up with evolutionary design is easier as well. We seek feedback in two ways. One, we use unit tests to make sure the code meets the programmer's expectations. Two, we hold regular demos and seek customer feedback. In between demos, we constantly interact with customers to get their input and feedback. What's courage? It's not about calling the tall, big guy ugly. It's about not hesitating to admit you may have to throw away what you've done to make things simpler or easier to work with. It's about being able to bring attention to problems that may benefit from reworking, even if that means admitting you didn't get it right the first time.

XP insists on having on-site customers, recommends a two-to-three-week iteration cycle, and de-emphasizes documentation.

XP takes the practices that produce results and takes them to extremes:

- *Refactoring.* Because agile development favors evolutionary design and change is inevitable, the code should be kept simple, understandable, and maintainable. Refactoring helps this by removing duplication, by removing unnecessary complexity, and by making the code more cohesive.

- *Simple design.* Some of us have a tendency to build complexity into our applications. We say, "I need this feature to make the code extensible." Often this perceived extensibility ends up overly complicating our system. By keeping the design simple—striving for "simple design that works"—we make the code easier to maintain and make it easier for the design to evolve. Ron Jeffries emphasizes this in his YAGNI principle by stating that "you aren't gonna need it." This means postponing features until you clearly see the need for the added complexity. It's a pay-as-you-go model.

- *Paired programming.* code review is good, why not do it all the time? A pair of programmers works together developing code; while one person is writing code, the other is thinking about its correctness, evaluating what unit tests may be written, thinking of simpler ways to express the ideas, and so on.

- Collective Ownership: You probably have worked on a project where you've been told, "No matter what you do, don't touch that piece of code. The guy who wrote it is no longer here and no one understands how it works," That's scary.

  How does code get that way? It happens when a programmer becomes isolated and his code is kept from the view of others. Collective ownership eliminates this problem. Since others look at your code, you keep it clean and understandable. Anyone on the team who understands the code can change it or fix a bug. This is a way to reduce the impact of losing people from a project. You can also effectively reallocate resources.

- *Coding standards.* Collective ownership is possible only if the code can easily be understood and modified by different team members. Following a consistent coding standard helps with this. Without a coding standard, developers may get frustrated looking at code, or they may spend too much time modifying the appearance of the code instead of working with it. Coding standards go beyond the question of where you put the curly braces. It is about naming conventions and other guidelines your team can agree upon.

- *Unit testing.* We all make mistakes, and our minds play tricks on us from time to time. So seek feedback from the code to make sure what you typed actually meets your expectations. Unit testing provides a safety net for you when you refactor your code and make enhancements—after all, breaking what already works doesn't help.

- *Continuous integration.* You have good unit tests, and you run them every time you modify your code. However, what if your change breaks your colleague's expectations? You may not find out for days, and by the time the problem surfaces you've moved on to other tasks. If you're like me, you'll have forgotten critical details about the code.

  So it's critical to minimize the time between making the change and getting feedback about its impact. After all, if your code sucks, you'd rather hear it from your computer rather than your co-worker, right? Continuous integration tools constantly pick up your code, compile it, and report the health of the code. You can configure it to send out different levels and frequency of notification. You take proactive steps to make sure your code stays healthy at all times.

- *Metaphor.* You improve communication and guide your team's development effort by sharing a common set of stories of how the whole system works.

- *The planning game.* You plan and scope your releases by considering the business values and priorities and by making technical estimates. You follow a realistic, adaptive plan, and you're happy to change plans as you go along. You care more about succeeding than sticking with a predefined plan.

- *Small releases.* Big-bang releases often shock customers. They also increase your risk. So, focus on developing and delivering small chunks of functionality and getting feedback to steer the progress of further development.

- *On-site customers.* Success depends heavily on interaction and collaboration. We want to discuss the details, get input from customers, and make sure what we're developing is relevant and meets their expectations. Such constant interaction necessitates having a customer on-site—meaning, in the same room—so we can approach them at any time.

- *40-hour work weeks.* After a certain point, our productivity is inversely proportional to the number of hours we work. We make fewer mistakes when we're fresh and not overworked. XP recommends that you don't work overtime two weeks in a row.

Pros and Cons

XP works effectively for smaller (20 people or fewer) teams. It is not for all teams. The business culture of your team decides whether this is the right approach for you. Is your team goal-oriented or paperwork-oriented? Do people care about the amount of work completed or the number of hours spent? Are the members of the team flexible and open to change? Is the technology you use lightweight—is it adaptable to change, or does it bog you down? Does your work environment promote interaction and collaboration?

XP discourages documentation. This has advantages and disadvantages. It makes it easier to keep up with rapid change. However, when your team is nearing completion of a project and you want to hand over the maintenance of your project to someone else, it gets hard—they're left with code and a whole lot of nothing else. Documentation in moderation—keeping in mind what the purpose is and where readers can get more information, often from code—is better than no documentation at all.

Scrum

Scrum was developed by Ken Schwaber and Jeff Sutherland (*Agile Project Management with Scrum* [Sch04]). The term comes from the game of Rugby; a *scrum* is a group effort to quickly move to counter the opposing team, adjusting the momentum along the way.

Features

Scrum relies on self-directed and self-organized teams. A Scrum *master* acts as a coach, keeping distractions out and facilitating and coordinating the team. Each iteration, called a *sprint*, lasts 30 days. No work is added in the middle of a sprint, and a demo to the stakeholders is held at the end of the iteration. Backlogs and burn-up charts help with adaptive planning. Daily, short, stand-up meetings are used to keep everyone informed. At these meetings you tell the team what you worked on the day before, what your goal for the day is, and what's holding you back. The team works together in determining the success criteria for the sprint and realizing that goal. The key values of Scrum are commitment, focus, openness, respect, and courage. The team is (or is expected to be) committed to realizing the goals of the project, avoiding obstacles along the way. The team is focused and keeps the distractions away. The overall status of the project, along with each individual's status, is kept in the open for anyone to view. The team members take responsibility for their actions instead of trying to fix blame.

Pros and Cons

Scrum focuses more on planning and executing a project—an essential part of software development. It is somewhat light on programming practices. Although Scrum does not discourage documentation, it recommends that you do only what's necessary.

Evo

Evolutionary Project Management (Evo), developed by Tom Gilb, is one of the oldest methodologies.

Features

Evo is averse to big, up-front specification. Evo recognizes that understanding the requirements and developing the design are both evolutionary. It recommends working with a short list of project objectives. The duration of an iteration is (an aggressive) five days, emphasizing measurable progress and frequent delivery to stakeholders.

Pros and Cons

Evo works hard to avoid certain project risks. The five-day iteration is good for a short duration (three-month-long) projects. However, for longer project durations, this may result in team burnout. It also suggests a language for specification that may appear somewhat burdensome.

Crystal Family

The Crystal family of methods was developed by Alistair Cockburn (see *Crystal Clear: A Human-Powered Methodology for Small Teams* [Coc04]).

Crystal comes in different flavors (actually, colors)—you pick one based on the criticality of your project.

Features

The Crystal family comes in four colors: clear, yellow, orange, and red. You pick the one based on the project team size and criticality—the Crystal color is a metaphor for difficulty. You start with a lighter color and move to a darker color only when your project shows significant signs of risk. It emphasizes people and communication. Criticality is based on the potential losses due to defects; factors include loss of comfort, discretionary money, essential money, and life. Crystal asks teams to reflect and improve and to criticize and fix. It encourages open communication and promotes honesty and criticism. It recognizes that feedback is essential, and teams need to be fast. Crystal requires expert users to consult with. The usual agile programming practices are recommended as well.

Pros and Cons

Crystal recognizes that there is no one solution for all problems or projects. However, not all colors are fully defined.

Lean Development (LD)

Lean development was developed by Robert Charette based on Toyota's Lean Manufacturing model (see *Lean Software Development: An Agile Toolkit for Software Development Managers* [PP03]).

Features

LD emphasizes satisfying customers, promoting project reversibility, providing business value, and creating minimum yet essential solutions. It defines phases for start-up, steady-state, and transitional-renewal. It encourages you to focus on completing a project more than constructing it (buy instead of build, if you can).

Pros and Cons

LD focuses on high-level strategic business processes. It states that development is a team effort and that pushing the approach beyond its limits will not yield results. It also emphasizes that need should determine the technologies used.

Adaptive Software Development (ASD)

ASD was developed by Jim Highsmith and Sam Bayer based on rapid application development (*Adaptive Software Development* [III99]).

Features

ASD emphasizes continuous adaptation of process, collaboration, and learning. It recommends iterative, risk-driven, change-tolerant development. The development effort is mission-based and feature-driven.

Pros and Cons

ASD does not dictate how to do things or what specific practices to follow. It establishes general guidelines, giving you the flexibility to figure out your own way to achieve your goals.

12.4   Which Methodology Should You Use?

We have looked at half a dozen agile methodologies. Which one should you choose?

Any methodology that becomes dogmatic fails. Sometimes it makes sense to use a certain practice, and sometimes it may not apply to your particular setting or project. Although XP deals with a number of tactical issues, it does not cover enough of project planning and management. Scrum, on the other hand, addresses those issues but does not fully address some of the programmer-specific issues. Evo has some nice ideas about keeping your specification and design evolutionary.

The best methodology is the one that works for you. It is your responsibility to learn the different practices. However, it is more important to understand the reasons behind these practices. Learning the whys more than the hows helps you to make prudent and pragmatic decisions as to what combination of practices will be of use to help in specific situations and projects. I would rather use a mixture of practices that provide direct benefits than stick with all the practices of one particular methodology. I like the freedom to choose. You have that choice as well.

Chapter 13

The Many Guises of Method Instrumentation

by Eitan Suez

Eitan Suez is a programmer living and working in Austin, Texas. He has been programming in Java since 1995 and is a Certified Java Programmer. Eitan is the author of an open source Java documentation system named Ashkelon (see http://ashkelon.sourceforge.net/) and, more recently, of the jMatter framework for extremely agile software construction for workgroups. Eitan speaks at the No Fluff Just Stuff series of programming symposia on a variety of topics including Java documentation systems, Cascading Stylesheets, NakedObjects, Hibernate, and more. Eitan is active with his local Java Users Group and maintains weblogs at http://java.net and http://u2d.com.

Eitan lists his favorite books and tools starting on page 220.

I have been involved with NFJS, on and off, for a while. I recall NFJS's first show in Austin, Texas, where I had the opportunity to speak on my open source project, Ashkelon, and to meet other speakers including Jason Hunter and James Duncan Davidson. It has been maybe four years since then, and I've personally participated in roughly two dozen symposia.

One of the talks I am giving in 2006 focuses on the excellent Hibernate O/R mapping framework.[1] There are many challenges to giving an effective talk, one that teaches well and imparts good, solid information to attendees in 90 minutes. One method (and one that I have come to really enjoy, though it requires much preparation) is to spend just a little time flipping from slide to slide and as much time as possible doing group coding sessions, where you attempt to expose as much of an API or framework in a meaningful sample application. This mode turns a passive presentation into an active one: attendees become engaged in solving a problem.

Ruby on Rails is a terrific candidate for a great talk because it lends itself well to this mode of presentation. You don't have to spend tedious and precious minutes in front of an audience hacking XML configuration files just to get a "hello, world"–calibre demo up and running. Instead, you get to work showing the relevant aspects of the task you have to perform and show meaningful results in short order. "There he goes again with Ruby and Rails," you might be thinking. OK, so I chose a bad example. In the Java world, the NakedObjects framework is another perfect candidate for doing hands-on coding in front of an audience. I had the pleasure of giving talks on the topic of NakedObjects in 2005, and, let me tell you, we had a fantastic time with it (and I have the session evaluations to prove it! :-)).

So here's my question: is it possible to do the same thing for a talk on Hibernate? You bet! Let's explore that together. Here is what I am promising you in return: we're going to end up coding a pretty cool, reusable little framework. In the process, we're going to have a lot of fun connecting the dots between all kinds of technologies including Hibernate, JUnit, the Spring framework, Java 5 features including annotations and varargs, and finally aspect-oriented programming.

Are you ready? Let's begin by discussing the basic setup for a simple Hibernate tutorial. What ingredients will we need?

---

[1] http://www.hibernate.org

- A build file (build.xml)

- A log4j config file (log4j.properties)

- A Hibernate config file (hibernate.properties or hibernate.cfg.xml)

- A couple of model objects and their corresponding mapping files

- Some kind of utility class to load the Hibernate configuration and build a session factory

All of these are pretty standard for Hibernate. In fact, if you haven't ever looked at Hibernate, I highly recommend reading through Chapter 1 of the Hibernate 3.1 reference documentation, which is a simple tutorial that walks you through the specifics of writing each file.

I won't walk you through the specifics of each and every file. The log4j config file is not strictly necessary but is practically de facto. In a Hibernate talk, we can safely think of it as a black box. Ant has likewise become so commonplace and indispensable that it is essentially a prerequisite today for doing any Java-related work.

The interesting nuggets in teaching Hibernate (in my opinion, of course) include the following:

- Understanding the mapping files and how to write them

- Learning HQL, the Hibernate Query Language

- Discovering Hibernate's wonderful (IMHO) Criteria API

- Looking at the nuances of the Hibernate run-time API, detached objects, the roles of the SessionFactory and Session objects, transactions, and so on

- Discovering the beauty of object-oriented queries and persistence modeling; you can perform polymorphic queries, model inheritance, and do away with the object-relational impedance mismatch

So, again, let's repeat the question: how do we structure a talk on Hibernate such that an audience spends very little time on the setup and configuration and much time on those nuggets I just listed?

Here are a few items that, if made part of one's setup, could get us there:

- Being able to easily rebuild or update the database schema from the model and mapping files (schema-export and schema-update).

- Using a Spring-like HibernateTemplate mechanism to avoid having each example repeat boring setup and teardown code that accompanies each hibernate test run: get a session, begin a transaction, commit the transaction, and close the session.

- When learning Hibernate, I expect to be doing many "one-off" tests, testing how changes to an HQL query affect the obtained results, and so on. I should have an easy way to build a bunch of Hibernate "tests," a simple way to add tests, and an easy way to control which test I want to run at a particular moment in time.

- It would also be nice to have some of the fixture support that Rails has to prepopulate a test database.

In this chapter, we're going to attack the first three.

13.1 Easy Schema Exports and Schema Updates

The first item, having the ability to easily rebuild a schema, is provided by Hibernate. One way to do this is to turn on the hbm2ddlauto feature in the configuration, which can be used to automatically drop and re-create our tables during each run. This could work, though you don't always want to do this on each run. For example, if you just tested a query and simply want to run another query, rebuilding the schema would simply take extra time and add lots of noise to the output. I prefer using Hibernate's SchemaExport and SchemaUpdate tools directly. These come in two flavors: you can use them as Ant tasks in your Ant build file, or you can call them programmatically. It really doesn't matter which you use. I like to have that capability exposed in both environments. Here's how I've set things up.

In the utility class where I build my session factory (let's call it HibernateUtil), I add these methods:

```
public static void schemaExport()
{
  SchemaExport tool = new SchemaExport(config);
  tool.setDelimiter(";");
  tool.create(true, true);
}
public static void schemaUpdate()
{
  SchemaUpdate tool = new SchemaUpdate(config);
  tool.execute(true, true);
}
```

I then expose these methods to the command line with a main method:

```java
public static void main(String[] args)
{
   if (args == null || args.length != 1)
   {
      System.err.println("Usage: java utils.HibernateUtil [export|update]");
      System.exit(0);
   }

   if ("update".equals(args[0]))
   {
      schemaUpdate();
   }
   else if ("export".equals(args[0]))
   {
      schemaExport();
   }
}
```

Then, in my Ant build file, I can use the *<java>* task to invoke that main method:

```xml
<target name="schema-x" depends="compile">
  <java classpathref="class.path" fork="true"
        classname="util.HibernateUtil">
    <arg value="${arg}" />
  </java>
</target>
```

I could invoke this target directly from the command line with the following:

```
ant schema-x -Darg=update|export
```

However, I'd prefer something like this:

```
ant schema-export
```

and this:

```
ant schema-update
```

This is easily accommodated with two more targets:

```xml
<target name="schema-export" description="export schema">
  <antcall target="schema-x">
    <param name="arg" value="export" />
  </antcall>
</target>

<target name="schema-update" description="update schema">
  <antcall target="schema-x">
    <param name="arg" value="update" />
  </antcall>
</target>
```

OK. That was really simple. And we didn't really have to do any work since Hibernate gives us the export and update tools, and we just invoke them. The important thing is that during a lecture, I now have the flexibility of updating my schema whenever necessary with a minimum of fuss and, more important, a minimum amount of time.

13.2 Avoiding Tedious Setup and Teardown Code

Let's start by understanding the problem. Here is some code, taken directly from the Hibernate 3.1 reference documentation (Chapter 1, "Intro to Hibernate"):

```
private Long createAndStoreEvent(String title, Date theDate)
{
    Session session = HibernateUtil.getSessionFactory().getCurrentSession();
    session.beginTransaction();

    Event theEvent = new Event();
    theEvent.setTitle(title);
    theEvent.setDate(theDate);

    session.save(theEvent);
    session.getTransaction().commit();

    return theEvent.getId();
}
```

We can distinguish between two types of code in this method: static (boilerplate) code that must be invoked before and after the code that is directly relevant to this creating and storing the event. For each new method we add, we're going to have to repeat the before and after parts. We'll have code duplication.

In languages such as Smalltalk, Ruby, and JavaScript, refactoring our code is fairly straightforward. Just for fun, let's try to do this refactoring in JavaScript. Here's how things might (fictitiously) look in JavaScript before the refactoring:

```
function createAndStoreEvent(title, date)
{
  var session = getSessionFactory().getCurrentSession();
  session.beginTransaction();
  var event = new Event(title, date);
  session.save(event);
  session.getTransaction().commit();
  return event.getId();
}
```

And, here is how it might look after refactoring:

```
function createAndStoreEvent(title, date)
{
  return doInSession(function(session)
  {
    var event = new Event(title, date);
    session.save(event);
    return event.getId();
  });
}
function doInSession(codeBlock)
{
  var session = getSessionFactory().getCurrentSession();
  session.beginTransaction();

  var result = codeBlock(session);

  session.getTransaction().commit();
  return result;
}
```

The previous code creates an anonymous function (that takes a session parameter) and passes that function as an argument to the doInSession() method. The anonymous function is called a *functor*, and the function that wraps it is called a *higher-order function*. In JavaScript, functions are objects that can be passed around and invoked later. The doInSession() method invokes our code block on the following line:

```
var result = codeBlock(session);
```

In Java, we can think of the java.lang.reflect.Method class as being somewhat analogous to that code block. It's an object, so we can pass it around. And we can invoke it later using Method.invoke(). The code just ends up not looking as clean as the JavaScript version.

One of the main things that frameworks such as Spring do for Hibernate is provide this type of refactoring, similar to what we just did in JavaScript. The Spring framework defines an interface, HibernateCallback, with the following single method signature:

```
Object doInHibernate(Session session)
  throws HibernateException, SQLException;
```

This interface is analogous to the JavaScript anonymous function we passed around. Spring then defines the HibernateTemplate.execute() method; here's the complete method signature:

```
public Object execute(HibernateCallback action)
  throws DataAccessException;
```

Clients can now invoke execute() like this:

```
// Assume the containing class has a reference to a hibernateTemplate variable
private Long createAndStoreEvent(final String title, final Date theDate)
{
  return hibernateTemplate.execute(new HibernateCallback()
    {
      public Object doInHibernate(Sesssion session)
      {
        Event theEvent = new Event();
        theEvent.setTitle(title);
        theEvent.setDate(theDate);
        session.save(theEvent);
      }
    });
}
```

We delegate the responsibility of ensuring that the proper setup() and teardown() code is invoked to Spring's HibernateTemplate.

We don't really need to use the Spring framework to do this. We could have written our own equivalent. The point is that the code duplication has now been removed. We're back to a more refactored situation.

Still, I'm not really happy with the way things are. I still have to tediously set up an anonymous inner class each time I want to invoke some Hibernate code. Can the situation be improved further? HibernateTemplate does give us other utility methods such as executeFind() that improve the situation.

Let's go in a different direction. I seem to have been using terminology from JUnit: setUp() and tearDown() are JUnit methods. Furthermore, JUnit does appear to be doing something similar to what we want, though in a different context. JUnit will invoke a bunch of methods for us; it harvests those methods whose names are prefixed with test from a given class. It then uses each essentially as a code block that it invokes in isolation from the other methods.

Can we use JUnit for what we're trying to do? You bet.

13.3 JUnit

What does JUnit do when it runs your tests?

This is a very interesting question, because the way things *look* when we're writing our test classes and the way they *work* are very different. (I recently looked at a JUnit alternative, TestNG. It is another fairly popular testing framework that employs Java 5 annotations. TestNG was motivated by its author's frustration that the way things look and work in JUnit are indeed very different from one another.)

For a given class, say MyTest, with a given set of test methods—test1(), test2(), and test3()—what does JUnit do? Here's the answer, in pseudocode:

```
for each test in tests:
  setUp();
  run test;
  tearDown();
```

Compare that to what we want to do with Hibernate:

```
for each hibernate test:
  setup the session, begin a transaction
  run the test
  commit the transaction, close the session
```

So, in the lecture environment, we don't have to use Spring to talk about Hibernate. All we have to do is set up a simple JUnit test:

```java
public class HBMTest extends TestCase
{
    Session session;

    protected void setUp() throws Exception
    {
        session = HBMContext.getSessionFactory().getCurrentSession();
        session.beginTransaction();
    }

    protected void tearDown() throws Exception
    {
        session.getTransaction().commit();
        session.close();
    }

    public void testQueryEvents()
    {
        List events = session.createQuery("from Event e").list();
        System.out.println(events.size() + " Events in database");
    }

    public void testQueryPeople()
    {
        List people = session.createQuery("from Person p").list();
        System.out.println(people.size() + " People in database");
    }
}
```

Can it be that two things we don't normally think of as related to one another essentially solve the same problem? It seems that Spring and JUnit do have something in common.

13.4 One More Time, Just for Fun

Rather than use an external framework such as Spring or JUnit, let's write one ourselves. I happened upon Elliotte Rusty Harold's relatively recent article on IBM's developerWorks titled "An early look at JUnit 4."[2]

One of the main themes of JUnit 4 is a move away from method naming conventions to Java 5 annotations. I must admit annotations seem to be a better solution than method naming conventions for tagging methods. For those of you not familiar with the new flavor that JUnit 4 brings to the table, the basic gist can be illustrated with the following quick code snapshots. Here's the "before" picture:

```
public void testSomething()
{
  assertTrue(someBoolean);
}
```

And the "after" picture:

```
@Test public void iCanBeNamedAnything()
{
  assertTrue(someBoolean);
}
```

My experiments with annotations in the last few months make at least one thing clear: defining, implementing, and wiring up annotations in Java 5 is simple and easy; it's actually a joy. I propose we write an annotation-based solution similar to JUnit 4 as a means of running code blocks that require some kind of standard, repetitive setup and teardown (or before and after) treatment.

Let me explain more specifically what I'd like to do. What if I, the developer, supplied the following pieces:

- My "tests":

  ```
  @ContextInfo(HBMContext.class)
  public class HBMTests
  {
  ```

```
    @Test public void storePerson(Session session)
    {
        Person p = new Person("Eitan", "Suez", 35);
        session.save(p);
    }

    @Test public void fetchPeople(Session session)
    {
        List people = session.createQuery("from Person p").list();
        // iterate over people or whatever..
    }
}
```

- A Context, or harness in which to run these "tests":

```
public class HBMContext implements Context
{
    public void runTest(Block block)
    {
        Session session = getSessionFactory().getCurrentSession();
        session.beginTransaction();

        block.call(session);

        session.getTransaction().commit();
        session.close();
    }
}
```

I want machinery that will wire all this together for me. This machinery would be passed a class containing the tests, and it would go looking for the methods tagged with the @Test annotation and run each in turn in the supplied context; it would invoke HBMContext.runTest() on my behalf for each "test" method.

Finally, how about we invoke our machinery with something like this?

```
new Runner(HBMTests.class).run();  // run all "tests"
```

And why not this, too?

```
new Runner(HBMTests.class).run("fetchPeople");  // run only a single test
```

13.5   The Implementation

Let's start with the easiest part: defining the annotations:

```
@Retention(RetentionPolicy.RUNTIME)
public @interface Test {}
```

There's nothing to the Test annotation. It's simply a marker annotation. The only pesky part is having to explicitly mark the retention policy.

The ContextInfo annotation is almost as simple. We need to allow the class under test to specify what context it wants to be run in by specifying its class name:

```
@Retention(RetentionPolicy.RUNTIME)
public @interface ContextInfo
{
  public Class value();
}
```

We also need to define an interface for implementing various contexts:

```
public interface Context
{
  public void runTest(Block block);
}
```

Notice that I've taken the liberty of defining a method call wrapper named Block. Here's that interface:

```
public interface Block
{
  public void call(Object... params);
}
```

The cool part here is what Java 5's varargs feature buys me: flexibility. I don't have to hard-code the method signature; it can remain very generic.

We're halfway there. Here's a quick and dirty implementation for a Block, the MethodBlock class:

```
public class MethodBlock implements Block
{
    private Object _instance;
    private Method _method;

    public MethodBlock(Object instance, Method method)
    {
        _instance = instance;
        _method = method;
    }

    public void call(Object... params)
    {
        try
        {
            _method.invoke(_instance, params);
        }
```

```
            catch (IllegalAccessException e)
            {
                e.printStackTrace();
            }
            catch (InvocationTargetException e)
            {
                e.printStackTrace();
            }
        }
    }
```

MethodBlock is given a method and an instance to call the method on.
When I invoke call() on it, it turns around and invokes its method.

Finally, let's write the Runner machinery:

```
public class Runner
{
    private Context _context = null;
    private Map<String, Block> _blockMap = new HashMap<String, Block>();

    public Runner(Class<?> instrumentedClass)
    {
        ContextInfo contextInfo = instrumentedClass.getAnnotation(ContextInfo.class);
        Class contextClass = contextInfo.value();

        Object instrumentedInstance = null;
        try
        {
            _context = (Context) contextClass.newInstance();
            instrumentedInstance = instrumentedClass.newInstance();
        }
        catch (InstantiationException e)
        {
            throw new RuntimeException("Failed to instantiate test and/or context class");
        }
        catch (IllegalAccessException e)
        {
            throw new RuntimeException("Failed to instantiate test and/or context class");
        }

        Method[] methods = instrumentedClass.getDeclaredMethods();

        for (int i=0; i<methods.length; i++)
        {
            if (methods[i].isAnnotationPresent(Test.class))
            {
                MethodBlock block = new MethodBlock(instrumentedInstance, methods[i]);
                _blockMap.put(methods[i].getName(), block);
            }
        }
    }
}
```

```java
public void run()
{
    for (Block block : _blockMap.values())
        _context.doInContext(block);
}

public void run(String blockName)
{
    Block block = _blockMap.get(blockName);
    _context.doInContext(block);
}

}
```

Let's analyze this code one step at a time. For a given class containing our code blocks, here is what Runner needs to do:

1. Look up the @ContextInfo annotation to figure out what Context class to run the code blocks in.

2. Instantiate a context, in anticipation of calling runTest() on it.

3. Instantiate the instrumented class, in anticipation of calling each of its methods.

4. Harvest the @Test-tagged methods on the instrumented class.

5. Tuck away the list of code blocks in a map in anticipation of fulfilling its run() and run(blockname) method obligations.

As you can see, the implementation is quite straightforward and simple. I took the liberty of using Java 5 generics in this case (*read with a Texas drawl:* figured I might as well since I was already in Java 5 land).

13.6 Reflections

We now have a simple way to cook up a small Hibernate test or demo and run it. We can do the following:

- Run a bunch of tests (not sure yet whether/why I'd want to do that in a Hibernate context)

- Liberally add and remove @Test tags on methods to control the set that I want to run at a given time

So, we have the flexibility we were looking for when we set out to have a good setup for teaching Hibernate:

- We can update our schema when necessary.

- The clutter of creating anonymous CallBack interfaces is gone.

- We can play with HQL or parts of the Hibernate API with a minimum of fuss; we can run one-off tests whenever we want.

We can use either JUnit with setup() and teardown() methods or cook up our own little framework. Here's what I like about the code we wrote for ourselves:

- By actually writing the machinery, we now know what happens behind the scenes. There's no more guessing. There's no better way to understand the the way something works than by attempting to write it ourselves.

- We discovered that it took little code and little time to set up our own mechanism.

- We should have also gotten a good feel for a situation where annotations really shine. The parts of our system that called for annotations included the following:

  - The need to relate (or link) our test class to a specific running context (via the @ContextInfo annotation)

  - The need to tag methods (with the @Test marker annotation)

13.7 AOP

In a way, what JUnit does is akin to a mini-AOP framework. With JUnit, we have the ability to instrument methods by specifying what code should be run before and after the method is invoked. The same can be said of the code we wrote: we've implemented the ability to instrument methods tagged with a marker annotation. And we can specify how these methods are instrumented by implementing Context classes (the runTest() method).

It turns out that a tool such as AspectJ is, in a sense, a more complete solution to this general issue:

- Through pointcuts, we are given powerful mechanism for picking out which methods to instrument.

- Through the various advice methods, we have the ability to inject code before(), after(), and around() a method and to invoke the method itself with proceed().

You could think of JUnit's setUp() and tearDown() methods as mere aliases for before() and after() advice on test methods. Rather than taking a few more pages to look at AspectJ in detail, I'd like to invite you to attend an upcoming NFJS symposium near you and to hear our resident expert on AOP, Ramnivas Laddad, give you the low-down.

Summary

In many situations, the way to eliminate code duplication is by passing code as an argument to another piece of code: by using functors and higher-order functions. These features exist natively in languages such as JavaScript, Smalltalk, and Ruby.

In Java, we discover that many of the frameworks we use provide their own mechanisms to address the same problem. The same pattern exists in many guises, and is veiled behind different semantics and different metaphors.

In this article, I discussed JUnit, AspectJ, and Spring implementations of the Template and Callback patterns for Hibernate and other frameworks it wraps. Here are some I did not specifically discuss: Spring AOP, EJB3 interceptors, and emerging Java functors libraries including JGA[3] and Jakarta Commons Functor.[4]

---

[3]http://jga.sourceforge.net/
[4]http://jakarta.apache.org/commons/sandbox/functor/

Chapter 14

CSS: A Programmer's Perspective

by Eitan Suez

Eitan's bio appears on page 175.

Although it is certainly not always the case, it seems to me that web application shops polarize into two camps. On the one hand, there's the *designer/artist* camp that concentrates on the client side and its *look and feel*. On the other hand, there's the developer camp that has somewhat retreated to the server side, and concentrates on the serious issues of high availability, transactional integrity, and other ACID[1] things (J2EE).

Cascading Style Sheets   I've seen Cascading Style Sheets (CSS) championed not by programmers but by "designers" (for lack of a better term). Designers wield CSS to improve the state of the art in online publishing from a soup of tricks and hacks into something that is somewhat manageable and clean (let's resist the tendency, however, to replace HTML hacks with CSS hacks).

In the previous paragraph, I used the word *hacks*. What did I mean?

- The use of blank images as a poor man's spacer
- The (offensive) use of repeating nonbreaking spaces ( ), also for spacing
- The use of HTML tables to simulate the CSS box model (margins, borders, and padding)
- The use of HTML tables for layout and positioning (for which CSS provides an alternative)
- Font styling with *<font>* tags

What I see lacking, and where this modest article hopes to contribute, is in encouraging the use of CSS by programmers and developers:

- As a tool for *refactoring* the client side
- As a tool for exploiting modern browsers (such as Firefox) to their full potential
- Specifically, to take advantage of modern browsers' layout engines to reflow and restyle content dynamically (without having to consult the server)

Thus, I treat CSS here as a technology that is useful for client-side *developers*. This article is not about making a page look as nice as it can be; it's about making a web application's user interface as usable as it can be.

---

[1]ACID: Atomicity, Consistency, Isolation, and Durability

14.1 The Web 1.0

Yes, there was a time when sites were horrible, and I'm sure many sites still are horrible. Just look at the HTML source of the content. How legible is it? How easily can it be revised to give your content a different style or look?

It's usually easy to tell an old, pre-CSS site. These are the markers; the *code smells* (as Martin Fowler would say) of a site in need of an overhaul:

- Liberal use of nonbreaking spaces ( )
- Use of the deprecated *<font>* tag
- Blank GIF images used to generate margins and padding
- Nested HTML tables
- A high markup to content ratio
- Table rows with liberal use of colspan and rowspan attributes
- Empty table cells (used for their padding/margin side effects)

Of course, you don't have to really look for any of these smells. Your body will tell you: you'll get a nauseating feeling, or a feeling of immense frustration, maybe despair...but you'll know.

CSS gives us the necessary tools to transform such old sites into ones that are maintainable and easily revised. Moving a sidebar from one side of the screen to the other can be performed by replacing a float: left style declaration with float: right. But we need to remain cautious and make sure that when we use CSS, we are still moving in the direction of more readable and more maintainable code.

I've seen CSS employed in a way where the designer has to calculate the absolute position of a block in order to place it in a proper location. Such designs are fragile and expensive to keep up-to-date, because they require style changes when content changes.

How does one go about improving a pre-CSS site? One way to do it is to apply the principles of refactoring. I've recently employed refac- *refactoring* toring on a site that I maintain. You'd be amazed how much smaller, cleaner, and more readable the resulting site has become. I was able to make small, piecemeal changes over weeks, at my own pace. The look and behavior of the site was maintained throughout the process of cleaning up the markup. This particular site had been designed and implemented by someone else; making small, iterative changes worked well in this situation.

The other option, of course, requires a little more gumption but will often end up taking less time. Here is the recipe:

1. Extract the content from the existing site into a separate set of pages.

2. Make sure the content is complete and can be viewed in a plain old browser. Sure, it's lacking some style and layout and a look and feel, but that's coming.

3. Make some basic layout and look and feel decisions. Perhaps revise the structure of the content slightly to match the structure.

4. Link a new stylesheet into the header of the pages using either the *<link>* tag or @import CSS directive.

5. Start building the stylesheet. Begin with global styles: document margins, base font, and colors.

6. Proceed with any additional styling necessary to give specific types of blocks the look and positioning necessary to affect the end result.

7. As you go, you'll have a general idea of what you want to do. The feedback you'll get in the process of styling the document will help you make the finer, more detailed decisions.

I've employed this method to redesign a separate site. In this case, I didn't need to maintain the same look and feel, so it made more sense to start from scratch. Also, the former site had been created using automated WYSIWYG tools, which introduced a large amount of unnecessary markup, making it difficult to edit the existing content.

14.2   Refactoring Content?

A definition of refactoring, when applied to programming, is as follows:

A change made to the internal structure of software to make it easier to understand and cheaper to modify without changing its observable behavior[2]

When I apply the term *refactoring* to markup, I'm mentally substituting the following:

---

[2]A warm thanks to Martin Fowler for giving us the necessary terminology to express ourselves coherently and succinctly.

- *Software* with *markup and stylesheets and whatever other components that a web browser interprets to display our website*, and

- *Behavior* with *look, layout, style, and to some extent behavior, too*

So we're taking a site in its present (and possibly not-so-maintainable) state and making small, discrete, isolated changes. We test that the change did not break or change anything. Once we're satisfied, we can move on to the next small change. Over time, the entire site is slowly transformed into a clean, maintainable, even beautiful one.

Small (yet important) flaws may have been difficult to see because of the overwhelming amount of markup in the original version. Refactor, and they surface and are easily fixed. The pages become smaller and lighter. Browser parsing engines don't have as difficult a time loading our content. Fewer calls are made to the server to fetch a bunch of images. We discover that we didn't really need to make page *xyz* dynamic after all. It was an illusion, difficult to diagnose because of the complex structure of our site before we applied the refactorings. Indeed, the process of refactoring a site is interleaved with the process of evolving it and growing it.

14.3 Case Study: *I Inherited My Local JUG Site*

I admit it: like most JUG sites, our JUG site was really ugly. Our little community is thankful to one of our members for one day volunteering to redesign our site and give it a much improved, consistent look. It was a few months later that I inherited the duty of updating the content with new meeting information. I expected to find a modern, clean site. I was surprised when I opened the lid to find so many markup smells lying beneath.

I decided to refactor this particular site piecemeal. The main reason was simple: it was not a site I had designed. I didn't quite understand how the various effects were implemented. I didn't want to break anything.

Surprisingly, this site already contained a small stylesheet. I did the obvious thing first: I added global font styles it. Once I made sure that the global font styles properly applied to the text on the pages, I started removing <font> tags from the HTML. The DRY principle (Don't   DRY
Repeat Yourself) is at work here. Much refactoring in this domain has to do with removing duplication. In this case, we've got dozens—maybe hundreds—of font tags replaced with a single reference in a stylesheet.

CSS inheritance of font styles ensures that styles applied to parent elements also percolate to the children.

Next, I began looking for tables containing only a single column. The technique of employing tables for the task of simulating the CSS box model used to be rampant. In pre-CSS days, there was no alternative. Tables would be used just for the sake of applying padding, borders, and margins. With CSS, much markup in my pages was replaced with simple *<div>* tags. Each type of block needing a specific type of look would be categorized via the HTML class attribute and styled appropriately in my stylesheet. This attribute was added to the HTML specification specifically to accommodate CSS.

Nonbreaking spaces were all removed and their effects replaced with CSS margin and padding specifications. The same went for the *
* tag. References to blank images were removed and replaced with margins and padding as well.

I discovered a page that attempted to use tables to essentially simulate a float effect. I did away with table and replaced it with the CSS style property, designed specifically for such a layout task.

Sidebar elements were marked up consistently, and the styles for each list item were now applied uniformly. Another sidebar on the right side had the same problem: repetitive applications of the same styles were consolidated into a single set of rules that applied the style uniformly. The look of the site actually slightly improved. All margins between blocks were now uniform. The reason is simple: oftentimes, when the same style has to be applied repetitively, mistakes are made and quality suffers.

CSS allowed me to easily apply diagnostic borders to various blocks to gain insight into the structure of the pages. This insight in turn revealed ways to simplify structures and collapse tables, nested divs, and so on.

Once the minor stuff was cleaned up, I was now in a position to take a look at how some of the dynamic aspects of the site worked. There weren't many. The basic effect was the use of a single JSP that included a header, navigation bar, and content based on a parameter in the URL. Once I discovered that this was the only responsibility of the JSP file, I was able to consolidate two JSPs into a single file. I was able to eliminate a small but significant number of pages. I renamed pages to represent more clearly the content they carried and the role they

---

Before and After

If you're interested in actually reviewing the before/after pictures of this small site, I checked them into a CVS repository on http://austinjug.dev.java.net fairly early in the refactoring process. I wish I had made my CVS comments more specific instead of the useless "more cleanup" comment I usually went with. If you follow the above link, click "Version Control," then "Setup CVS command line client" for instructions on checking out the code. As for stats, I was able to make the site approximately 25% smaller, all the while adding content. But these figures highly depend on the quantity of content. A more useful figure would be the ratio of before to after markup, excluding the content (text). But I did not bother generating it.

---

played. I was now pleased that a directory listing yielded fewer files and more information.

I now knew where everything resided and where I needed to make a change. I had finally gotten to the point where the cumulative effects of my refactorings had created a site whose feel was distinctly better than its former state.

I continued refactoring in a similar fashion. I attacked other aspects of the site, one at a time. I inspected the construction of the site's header and undid its complexity. The process is akin to taking knots out of tangled rope. The original version used tables and table cell rowspan and colspan tricks to make the ends of the header rectangle appear to protrude on either side. I applied CSS relative positioning instead to reproduce the look. In this one case, although I was able to reproduce its original effect, I finally decided to deviate from the original design and ended up going with a simpler (yet still decent) look.

Wherever possible, I removed extraneous content or markup. Less was more. The personality of the site changed subtly. No one has commented on these site changes to me. I'm assuming no one has noticed them, a sign of good markup refactoring (changing the implementation without altering how the page looks).

Now, updating my local JUG's website takes me less time and is a much more, shall we say, *fragrant* experience.

14.4   Aspect-Oriented...Styling?

One of the aspects of CSS that really attracts me is its simplicity. It's a thread that CSS holds in common with HTML. One can learn HTML quickly, probably in a single day, without much *a priori* knowledge. CSS's syntax is clear and yet concise. But the real genius behind CSS is the realization that style is fairly orthogonal to content. Styling is an *aspect*, as in aspect-oriented programming (AOP).

aspect-oriented programming

pointcut

In AOP, a pointcut is defined as a program construct that selects join points. *Join points* are identifiable points in the execution of a program, such as a call to a method.

We could describe CSS's design using similar, analogous language. A CSS selector is the analog of the AOP pointcut. Instead of selecting join points, it selects identifiable points in a target document, such as a tag with an id. Like pointcuts, CSS selectors can select more than a single point. Any points matching the selector are returned.

In AOP, an *advice* is code that is executed before, after, or around a join point. Similarly CSS contains a list of styling declarations that are analogous to AOP's advice body. What's even more interesting is that CSS's *pseudoselectors* (:before, :after) are analogous to the ability in AOP to specify before and after advice.

The similarities abound. We can take this even further. CSS does not provide an :around pseudoselector. But that doesn't stop designers from coming up with their own simulations of the feature. Designers will often apply a display: none; style to the content of a block and yet slide in an image into the background of the containing block, thus essentially replacing content. This is analogous to AOP's around advice.

Having said all this, I'm no AOP expert—far from it. Although I've read about AOP, I have practically no experience in the field. But one can see that some aspects of AOP's design are quite evolved. AOP's design has more features compared to the design of CSS. It seems to me that we could evolve CSS by simply looking to what AOP has done and adopting those parts we lack and those parts we need in the web world.

So, let's get to it! What parts do we lack? What parts do we need? I think it'd be really cool to open the floodgates for a while and make accessible a number of features to experiment with, and then after we've collectively gained some experience and grown wiser, we can tighten up the features to only those that really prove to be valuable. It's somewhat analogous to a brainstorming activity.

So let's brainstorm a bit.

We can try to take the notion of pseudoselectors further. In addition to :before, and :after, we can introduce an :around or :replace. (Note: it turns out that CSS3 is adding a ton of new and powerful pseudoselectors).

We could also try to extend event pseudoselectors such as :hover to cover other things, such as :click.

We could even go as far as attempt to merge the syntax of AOP and CSS. Let's refactor the two designs into one. Let's make a sort of unified model for aspect design that applies to both code and XML documents.

Back down to earth: what if we could specify more than just styling in advice bodies? Technically we already do. CSS positioning allows us to inject positioning information.

Why not open CSS's advice bodies to things other than styling and positioning? Why not invoke code? This is what I'd like to see:

```
#some-id:click
{
  javascript:callMe();
}
```

That'd be pretty good for starters.

Status: this type of capability is already in the pipeline for CSS3. CSS3's module "behavioral extensions to CSS" is bundling in IE's HTC and element behavior (or Mozilla's analog: XBL) work. In addition, they'll be adding CSS-style event handling and code invocation (even the ability to embed a script within a CSS file with the @script directive).

The most intriguing thought here is the notion of using CSS's design as the basis for introducing some kind of AOP framework for JavaScript.

14.5 A More Semantic Web

Content tends to become more semantic as a consequence of employing CSS. Although the HTML tags become more abstract (<div>, <span>, <em>, and so on), the two magic HTML attributes, class= and id=, are in a sense a dynamic mechanism for creating one's own markup language.

Of course, this markup language can have anything from a horrible design to a superb one. It's up to the author to decide how extensive of a vocabulary to build.

Let's clarify what I mean with an example: take a catalog of books. If you were to come up with a markup language, you might end up with XML looking like this:

```
<book isbn="1234">
  <title>Cooking French</title>
  <author>John Doe</author>
  <abstract>blah..</abstract>
</book>
```

Now consider an HTML alternative:

```
<div class="book" id="1234">
  <span class="title">Cooking French</span>
  <span class="author">John Doe</span>
  <span class="abstract">blah..</span>
</div>
```

The ISBN could also have been specified as an invented attribute. It could have been made its own element. The <span>s could also have been <div>s instead. The point is that the new instruments of HTML, <div>, <span>, id=, and class= can be used as near equivalents to custom tags, all with the benefit of not having to define custom tags.

A major difference, of course, is that it's all loosely typed, so to speak. There's no XML schema for this custom HTML. One could say that the "new and improved" HTML is a mechanism for producing unofficial markup vocabularies.

Back to my original point, though: using CSS pushes you to structure your HTML in a manner similar to the previous example. What we end up with (besides cleaner content) is more semantic content, which is good and is something worth noting.

14.6   On the Nature of Web Applications

How is a web application different from a desktop application?

Web apps are more document-like. They're coarser grained. A web view (the page) will typically contain relatively larger amounts of information than a desktop application's view. This stems from the nature of web apps: they're remote and thus must be coarser grained—fewer round-trips to the server but fetching more information per trip.

This gives web applications a different feel from desktop applications. They also face different usability challenges. For example, all browsers I know support a word-processor *find* feature that lets you find a piece of text on a page. The browser will autoscroll to the proper location and highlight the matching text on the page.

Take the find feature in Mozilla. You can find something without taking your fingers off the keyboard. Simply typing the search characters automatically starts searching through the page. If the text is part of a hyperlink, then pressing `Enter` will have the same effect as clicking on that link.

Furthermore, techniques such as find don't all have to be generic. A web application developer can build little tools or UI widgets into the app that take advantage of the developer's knowledge of the application's domain to make the usability of the application really shine.

Fortunately for us, CSS features such as *visibility*, *font styling*, and *color coding*, can be employed with ease to provide a whole suite of such features.

I invite you to visit http://u2d.com/css/ and try the samples in the sidebar. Each is a user interface design pattern that exploits the various CSS properties to improve the usability of a web application.

Let's quickly discuss each sample:

Show/Hide Error

> Instead of displaying an error in its entirety, thus cluttering a page with lots of information that the end user may not be interested in, the error's details are hidden and summoned only at the end user's request by clicking a button. They're just as easily removed or hidden again.

Scrolling

> Sites are armed with headers, footers, sidebars, and menus for a very good reason. These areas are like the end user's cockpit controls. They need to be accessible at all times. Unfortunately, page bodies can be quite lengthy at times, and scrolling the main body often results in these controls scrolling out of view. The header or footer or sidebar links will often be clipped when the end user scrolls to view parts of the page body. Simply scrolling the body and not the rest of the page is the solution in this case.

Master/Detail

The epitome of the web-based catalog is the idea of viewing a list of entries and then being able to drill down to the specifics of a single item. In the case of the two round-trips to the server, one to fetch the listing and another to view the details, we don't have the issue of the details of a different item cluttering the user's locus of attention. But there are plenty of cases where both the listing and the details are on the same page (Javadoc springs to mind). A typical class page template will show the details of every method on a single page. The master/detail sample shows how to remove from sight anything but the one item that the user is interested in. Lots of information exists on that single page, yet the end user's view is a short, uncluttered page that quickly summons an item's details with a subsecond response.

Color Coding

Color coding is all about exploiting our natural ability to filter information. Most people can quickly parse and comprehend a fairly information-heavy page if that page is color-coded. There are many issues to address regarding color coding, including exploiting culturally or socially accepted conventions such as the color red implying an error or danger, for example.

Legends

Again, this sample is about making information available to the end user when requested and without requiring screen real estate.

Tabbed Panes

In this case, we're exposing (or hiding) information by category.

Dynamic Tables

This is another mechanism for filtering out information. In this case, the structure of the information is tabular.

Trees

Finally, the trees sample, which makes the branch nodes dynamically expandable, is more of the same: hiding information that the user is not interested in and enabling the end user's locus of attention on a portion of the tree.

What's really striking here is that all these features have the same common thread and solve the same general problem: that of distilling large amounts of content to help end users maintain their loci of attention.

These are all good things for web applications that begin to make them feel a little more like desktop applications.

14.7 Going Forward: My Wish List

A small wish list came out of my experience and experiments with CSS, a wish list for either improving CSS or for improving other aspects of the web by borrowing from the design of CSS:

- The ability to employ the same syntax that HTML framesets have regarding how to specify relative the allotment of space between two frames (horizontal or vertical), as in the following:

```
<frameset rows="10%,*" />
```

What I want is that little asterisk that allows me to tell the browser, "Give the remaining horizontal space to this block here."

- The extension of CSS's aspect-like design to scripting: using selectors to specify events upon which code is invoked, as follows:

```
a:click { javascript: doSomethingInteresting(); }
```

Status: this type of capability is already in the pipeline for CSS3, which contains a module called "behavioral extensions to CSS." This bundles IE's HTC and element behavior work. In addition, they'll be adding CSS-style event handling and code invocation (even the ability to embed script within a CSS file with the @script directive).

- The ability to reference a tag by id to specify relative positioning. That is, absolutely positioned elements are relative to the most immediate relatively positioned containing block. It'd be nice if I could place content at the bottom of the page but specify something like this:

```
#someContent
{
  position: absolute;
  relative-to: #someOtherContent;
}
```

- In CSS stylesheets selectors are analogous to XPath expressions that allow you to select or target specific points in a document. Programmatically, the DOM must be used to select such points. I think it'd be really nice if one could actually programmatically take advantage of the CSS selector "language" or "syntax," similar to the way we can use Xpath APIs.

Status: Version 1.5 of Prototype.js[3] adds this very feature!.

- In the same vein as the last request for a DOM getElementsBySelector() method, I wonder how they overlooked putting getElementsByClassName() into the DOM HTML API (on HTMLElement). Again, fortunately for us, Prototype.js has filled that gap.

- It would be really nice if the area where a list's list-style-type or list-style-image appears could be used as part of a selector in a CSS rule. That is, this area could be made into a "hot spot" for (for example) expanding and collapsing a tree. The current alternative is to target the entire list item, which is less than optimal.

---

[3]http://prototype.conio.net/

Chapter 15

Buried Treasure

by Glenn Vanderburg

Glenn Vanderburg has been a programmer through only the second half of the history of computing, but he's interested in the first 30 years, too. For years he has dreamed of teaching a course on the topic. That's just one reason he's delighted that people are discovering the practical value of knowing our history. Glenn is a consultant who lives in Plano, Texas, with his wife, Deborah, and their sons, James and Daniel.

Glenn talks about some recent tool and book favorites starting on page 221.

Over the past three years, many of my talks for the No Fluff, Just Stuff symposium series have shared a common theme. It was partly conscious, but mostly it came naturally, as a reflection of where I think our field is going.

I think our field is going backward.

And it's not a minute too soon. For years, we've been fighting our way forward, step by harried step, but for the most part it has been down the wrong path. The grass looked greener here—or at least, better manicured—but traps are lurking here, some of them very well concealed. We keep falling into them, but we keep fighting on. "We must be more careful!" we say, calling over our shoulders to our companions as we walk toward the next pit.

But some in the programming field have started to remember another place, one we passed on the way. It was a little unkempt and overgrown, to be sure, and maybe there were just as many dangers—but somehow the place, overall, was less dangerous. Plus, people who ventured in there keep telling us about the riches to be found in that place— wonderful treasures buried just below the surface.

The reasons *why* these older ways turn out to be better are subtle and occasionally complex, and I don't claim to understand them all. Whatever the reasons, the signs of what's happening are clear. Let's look at those first and then try to make sense of the whys and wherefores.

15.1 The Signs

The signs that we're returning to older stomping grounds are everywhere. Those of us programmers who know the history of our field spotted them early (although I certainly wasn't the first). Now they're so prominent, and growing so quickly, that many people have spotted the trend. The signs I've noticed tend to fall into a few distinct areas: the way we go about designing and building systems, the kinds of programming languages and techniques we employ, and the way languages and platforms are implemented.

Design

The way programmers and teams of programmers *design* software is changing. After decades of increasing investment in tools and disciplines to support an analytical approach to software design, our field is running headlong toward a more empirical approach based on itera-tion, trial and error, and rapid feedback. There is widespread acknowl-edgment that the task of software design is simply too complex to tackle with a purely analytical approach. Programming will always involve a lot of careful thought, of course, but we must also be guided by feed-back, checking our assumptions against the hard realities of real sys-tems and running code.

The modern approaches to design aren't precisely the same as the older approaches from the 1960s and 1970s, but they share many of the same characteristics. A prime example is the emphasis on iterative development. Long before it became fashionable to try to design a pro-gram completely before beginning programming, the common practice was to build a simple, working system and gradually enhance it. Sto-ries are even told of Marvin Minsky at MIT taking this practice to an extreme, beginning development by starting to debug an empty pro-gram. The modern equivalent of that, of course, is test-driven develop-ment. Guiding our development with automated tests is relatively new, but developing in small increments, evolving the design as we go, has a long history.

Another sign: today we are beginning once again to emphasize code over pictures in the design process. Don't get me wrong—we'll always draw pictures of our systems from time to time; that's something pro-grammers have always done. But as the centerpiece of the design pro-cess, UML and other graphical notations have clearly failed. After hav-ing tried for years to improve software design by focusing on graphical models before we start writing code, programmers have learned some-thing crucial. Code—good clean code, at least—is a more expressive notation for the details of software than boxes and lines.

As a computer science student in the 1980s, I read papers by Jon Bent-ley and others from Bell Labs extolling the virtues of domain-specific languages (DSLs). The best way to build many kinds of systems, they said, was to design simple, focused, special-purpose programming lan-guages for the applications' domains, implement those languages, and build the systems using languages tailored to the tasks at hand. Lan-guage development tools such as yacc and lex were introduced as tools to facilitate developing such languages. And that group had remarkable success practicing what they preached, building groundbreaking tools such as pic, grap, make, sed, awk, and, of course, yacc and lex. All of those tools are still in use, in some form or other, decades later.

That style of development never really took off outside Bell Labs. Now, though, it's seeing a sudden resurgence. One of the most dramatic overnight success stories in software development is the Rails web framework, and much of Rails' strength comes from its inclusion of several distinct, small domain-specific languages focused on various aspects of web application development. Two related tools that have also garnered their share of attention, Capistrano (née SwitchTower) and Rake, are also based on those concepts. The implementation techniques are different from what the Bell Labs gang wrote about (and I'll talk about the new techniques next) but the concepts are the same. The idea of domain-specific languages seems to be one whose time has come.

Programming Techniques

I also see big changes in the programming techniques we use to build our software. This isn't entirely unrelated to the previous section; these techniques have strong effects on our design, and vice versa.

The most obvious change in this category is the move toward dynamically typed languages. Static languages of various stripes have dominated the software development for decades, from the loosely typed C and C++ to the stronger type systems of Pascal, Java, and C#. Most programmers have been taught that strong, static typing and compile-time analysis provide the only way to build robust, reliable systems.

That idea seemed to make sense, but it ignored the many solid systems built using dynamic languages. Additionally, during my ten years as a Java programmer I saw firsthand that strong typing is not a panacea; in fact, truly robust Java-based applications are rather rare.

Today, many developers have realized that a static type system is a two-edged sword. It does have some benefits, but it also has some costs. The advent of unit testing, more than anything else, has served to weaken static typing's appeal. Ruby, Python, and even JavaScript are growing more and more popular as developers discover the productivity advantages of dynamic typing.

For various reasons, many of these dynamically typed languages are dynamic in other ways as well. Your code can change (or augment) the way built-in facilities work, for example. This sounds similar to how aspect-oriented programming systems work, but the idea isn't new; in fact, aspect-oriented programming is a direct attempt to adapt older dynamic language techniques to static languages, pioneered by some of the same people who built those dynamic language facilities.

Dynamic languages also blur the distinction between compile-time and run-time; in such languages, new code can easily be added to the system while it's running. Combined with other dynamic characteristics, this gives rise to a technique called *metaprogramming*, which is essentially extending your programming language from within. The practice of metaprogramming is a big part of the reason that domain-specific languages are making a comeback, because compared to building a stand-alone interpreter or compiler for a language, it's much, much easier to define domain-specific constructs in a language that supports metaprogramming. The new wave of DSLs gaining popularity in the Ruby community are built within Ruby itself as libraries.

The trend toward dynamically typed languages is both widespread and strong. Less obvious, though, is a resurgence of interest in functional programming and functional languages. Just in the past two years, two compelling applications have appeared that are written in Haskell: PUGS (an exploratory, prototype implementation of Perl 6) and Darcs (a powerful, decentralized revision control system). Other interesting systems have been written in Objective CAML (including MTASC, a free, blazingly fast ActionScript compiler). Those systems have prompted many programmers to learn those languages just so they can contribute to the projects, and the newcomers have been struck by the power and efficiency of functional languages.

Plus, interesting functional languages continue to appear. XQuery, the XML query language, is a functional language. This year's No Fluff, Just Stuff symposia will feature a talk from Ted Neward about Scala, a terrific functional language designed to work compatibly on both the JVM and the CLR. In fact, Ruby, Python, and JavaScript have strong functional characteristics and are often used in a functional style.

But it's not just a revival of old concepts in new languages; the old languages themselves are seeing a resurgence. A surprising number of people are discovering (or rediscovering) Lisp, due in part to the popular essays of Paul Graham. Also, the use of Smalltalk is growing again, sparked by some impressive systems such as Croquet and the brilliant Seaside web framework.

Language Implementations and Infrastructure

I remember vividly the reaction of many programmers when Java was released: "It's interpreted! It's garbage-collected! All array references are bounds-checked. You can't use languages like that; they're too slow!"

That was the common wisdom among most programmers for about three decades. To be efficient, languages had to be compiled, and programmers had to manage memory themselves.

It's true that many Java-based systems perform poorly, and Java to this day has a reputation for sluggishness. And, for that matter, early implementations of Java really were excruciatingly slow. But that was mostly due to immature implementations that used pure interpretation of bytecodes and naive garbage collection strategies. In modern Java-based systems, though, the slowness is due not to those characteristics of the language implementation but to the libraries, frameworks, and platforms that have been built on top of Java. Java's garbage collector performs extremely well, and many Java systems spend much less time managing memory than do equivalent C and C++ programs. As far as interpretation goes, the just-in-time compilers (JITs) and dynamic optimization technologies employed by most Java implementations produce very fast machine code at run-time.

Today we seem to have shed those earlier qualms about Java's style of language implementation. Oh, there will always be situations where C is the most appropriate technology, but for most of the systems we build, VM-based or interpreted languages are fast enough, and features such as automatic memory management and array bounds checking really do help us build more robust systems—they're much more helpful, in my opinion, than static typing.

For most systems, you get much more performance benefit from good architecture than you do from fast code. That's a big part of the reason that typical Rails applications are at least as fast as their J2EE counterparts, even though Java typically benchmarks as about ten times faster than Ruby.

15.2 Why Now?

So far I've avoided a crucial question: if these older ways of doing things are so great, why didn't they succeed at first? Lisp and Smalltalk had their moments, as did bottom-up and iterative development, and the market chose a different direction. Why? And what has changed now to make the time right?

First, it's important to realize that there are more ways to fail than there are to succeed, and the problems weren't necessarily inherent to the technologies. Here are just a few ideas about what went wrong the first time and why things are different now.

The kinds of design techniques and processes that are returning to prominence were originally used by individuals and very small teams and began to show real weaknesses on more ambitious projects with larger teams. It was perfectly natural to try to inject more "discipline" into things with the use of phases, careful analysis and planning, inspections, and so on. But there are other forms of discipline besides top-down control, and we've learned from painful experience that software development is just too complicated a task to really benefit from central planning. Economies around the world, successful businesses, and even military organizations are pushing power and responsibility down toward the people in the trenches. The software development industry has learned the same lessons. Rigid control hasn't helped us avoid mistakes, so the industry is returning to basic skills, communication, and cooperation, supported this time by powerful tools and improved team practices.

Dynamic languages can be implemented very efficiently, but it's not *easy* to do so. Early implementations of dynamic languages were rather slow and required a lot of resources. It was much easier to build a C compiler that generated fast code than to build, say, a Smalltalk VM that performed similarly well. But implementation techniques have continued to advance, and the performance gap has shrunk dramatically. Not every dynamic or functional language has a state-of-the-art implementation, but we know from examples like Common Lisp, Squeak Smalltalk, and Haskell that it is possible for such languages to be blazingly fast.

As language implementations have been getting faster, our cost models have been changing. The first time around, slow CPUs and expensive memory meant that computing resources were not to be wasted, and dynamic languages looked like the wrong trade-off. Now, though, the balance has shifted. Sure, we still can't afford to be completely heedless of CPU and memory utilization, but fast machines and cheap memory mean that the sensible trade-off today is very different. Productivity is much more valuable than it used to be in software development, and languages that save *our* time at the expense of some extra CPU cycles make a lot of sense.

As mentioned previously, we've begun using better development practices that help a lot. When projects don't use version control and don't have a disciplined approach to testing, the safety net offered by static typing seems to be quite valuable. We've learned, though, that we have to build our own safety nets that cover all aspects of the project, not just data types.

I could keep extending this list of reasons why things happened the way they did. The full list includes reasons such as primitive tools, fractured communities, weak development practices, incompatible competing dialects, expensive implementations, the lack of any free versions that developers could play with, and more.

Ultimately, though, we never really gave these tools and techniques a fair chance the first time. A world that hadn't yet really grasped the concept and power of "emergence" fled from iterative development as soon as it began showing flaws, not considering that the problem was a lack of supporting tools and practices rather than the technique itself. As far as languages are concerned, Lisp and Smalltalk were always on the fringes of the software field. COBOL, Fortran, C, and BASIC occupied the center. Occasionally we would adopt some of the ideas, such as object orientation, but we would try to fit them into the world we were used to, rather than taking them on their own terms. As a result, we missed some important subtleties, like (for example) the fact that object orientation doesn't exist in isolation but benefits greatly from other language characteristics such as blocks, dynamic typing, and automatic memory management.

So it's wrong to say "we tried that once and it failed." We're not going back to what *we* tried once; we're going back to what others had success with. The industry at large tried to go a different way, and at long last we've begun to realize that no matter how many new tools we throw at our problems, software development still isn't getting any easier. Maybe it's time to rethink the whole way we've been going. The people who really embraced Lisp and Smalltalk early on don't think those languages failed (except in terms of gaining broad acceptance). On the contrary, most of them that I know are either still finding ways to work with those technologies or else yearning for a return to the good old days.

15.3 More Past in Our Future

I predict that we'll see the increasingly wide adoption of dynamic languages, metaprogramming, and agile design and development practices over the next few years. In spite of many naysayers, momentum seems to be building in this direction.

I don't think it will stop with Ruby, Python, or any of the other new old languages that are gaining popularity. Although those languages borrow extensively from their progenitors, they stop short in some other ways. I love programming in Ruby, but occasionally I find myself needing some of the features of Smalltalk or Lisp that Ruby doesn't have—true macros, for instance, or the ability to easily pass multiple blocks to a single method (with appropriate cues as to their distinct roles). And don't get the idea that I'm an old Smalltalk or Lisp programmer! I come from a C, C++, and Java background. But I've recently begun to understand some of the subtle strengths of languages that I used to think were weird.

I'm not predicting a utopia, of course. These are trade-offs, and we'll give up some features to gain others. I can hear my skeptical friends asking now, "Sure, all that stuff is powerful, but is that the kind of power you want to give to the weakest programmers on your team?"

I bought into that argument for a while and argued that you should use truly powerful languages only with sharp, experienced teams. But then I started to notice something about the Java projects I was involved in: weak teams and weak programmers will go to great lengths to do the wrong thing. Time and again I've seen system designs that were not only inappropriate but also *much more difficult to build* than better designs would have been. I've just shaken my head in amazement—not at the inappropriate designs per se because good design is difficult but at the effort and tenacity it took to proceed with those designs in the face of the obstacles the teams had to overcome to build them.

What I've concluded is that you can't keep a weak team out of trouble by limiting the power of their tools. The way forward is not figuring out how to achieve acceptable results with weak teams; rather, it's understanding how to build strong teams and how to train programmers to be part of such teams. One place to start is with more emphasis on history. Our field is just barely 60 years old; there's no excuse for allowing programming students to remain ignorant of such recent history. Our history is rich with lessons that have been forgotten.

Here's an example. I'm developing with Rails right now, and Rails incorporates nice support for database migrations: little classes that encapsulate the changes to production databases (including both schema and data changes) required to move from one version or release of an application to another. It's a brilliant feature. But it has some problems, and most of them involve the way migrations mesh with the way we use version control. When we have a particular version of the software checked out, we are working with a set of files that describe the way the system looks at a given point in time. But migrations don't fit that model. There, in one version of your project, is a set of files that describe the whole history of the database schema, not just a point in time. It's like having a little version control system stored *within* your project, and that feels odd.

Typically we use version control to manage versions of program source code, and we use that source to build the system *from scratch* each time. Migrations, on the other hand, operate on persistent data; they don't have the luxury of starting from a clean slate.

In thinking about how to resolve some of these issues and perhaps fix them, I suddenly realized Smalltalk developers have dealt with similar issues for years. Smalltalk programs don't exist in source files on disk that are loaded, parsed, and compiled every time the system is run. Rather, they exist as objects—class objects, method objects, predefined and preconfigured instances, and other things—in a Smalltalk *image*, essentially a dump of Smalltalk's heap that is reloaded from disk and reconstituted just as it was the last time you were using it. In other words, Smalltalk programs exist as persistent objects.

So to learn how to solve my problems with migrations, it might help me to find out how Smalltalk developers do version management of their applications. I don't know the answer yet; that's a part of Smalltalk I'm not familiar with. But I'm going to find out.

There's more buried treasure there.

Appendix A

The Authors Speak!

We asked the authors to tell us what they're reading and which tools they're using. Here's what they said.

A.1 Scott Davis

Favorite Books

I've devoured a slew of non-computer-related books in quick succession: *The Tipping Point* [Gla02] and *Freakonomics* [LD05] are two great books that coincidentally explore some of the same case studies from different perspectives. Both are very accessible, enjoyable explorations of the phenomena of popularity. *The Tipping Point* is more of a psychology/sociology book whereas *Freakonomics* is written from the perspective of a PhD in economics. I'm hoping to gain some insight as to why some technologies like Ajax and Ruby on Rails aren't just merely interesting, but wildly popular. What is keeping something that I think is vastly superior (Mac OS X) from "crossing the chasm" to become a mainstream reality instead of a niche product?

The Paradox of Choice: Why More Is Less [Sch05] is another good book that is strangely complementary to the previous two. It talks about how, in theory, more choices should lead to happier consumers. In reality, study after study seems to indicate that the reverse is true—the more choices we have in a given category, the more unhappy we end up being about the choice we eventually make. The proliferation of web frameworks comes to mind here. Ajax frameworks seem to fall into this same category, while Ruby on Rails stands out as the clear market-leader for Ruby developers. Without taking anything away from the intrinsic beauty of Ruby on Rails, does the lack of competition contribute in some significant way to the infatuation with this framework? Will Ruby be as appealing to developers once it has the competitive, confusing, redundant ecosystem that Java has?

The last pure Java-related book I read was *Maven: A Developer's Notebook* [MO05]. Saying that Maven is just like Ant is a disservice to both. I haven't been drawn to Maven in the past because I felt like I was losing control of my build process. I'm slowly coming to the realization that it isn't a bug of Maven's; it's a feature. Ant allows me to micromanage every last detail of my build. Maven frees me from obsessing over the minutiae of my build process and allows me to produce working code more quickly. I haven't come to a conclusion on this matter yet, but *Maven: A Developer's Notebook* certainly makes the first strong argument I've heard that challenges the de facto standard of Ant.

Favorite Technical Tool

Probably Maven. Enough open source projects use it (ActiveMQ, Geronimo, GeoTools) that I can't ignore it any longer. It seems very Ruby on Rails–like in its ability to quickly set up a scaffolding (including unit tests) for a variety of Java projects and GEMS-like in its ability to "automagically" download required JARs for the build process. *Maven: A Developer's Notebook* [MO05] has gone a long way toward helping me understand Maven; now it's a matter of seeing whether I can actually incorporate it into my day-to-day Java development process.

I think that 2006 will be the year of JavaScript. As Glenn Vanderburg says, "JavaScript: There's a Real Programming Language in There." Ajax has gone a long way towards legitimizing the language. Bringing native Rhino support to the JVM in Java 6 means that JavaScript will be a first-class citizen in both the web browser as well as the JVM.

A.2 Neal Ford

Favorite Technical Book

A golden oldie, *Smalltalk Best Practice Patterns* [Bec96] by Kent Beck, is my favorite technical book. The Smalltalk guys already figured out most of the "innovations" we think we have discovered anew. Even if you don't care for Smalltalk, this book can teach you tons about software development.

Favorite Technical Tool

My favorite recent technical tool is actually a combination of a bunch of old technologies. In my current project, we needed to improve communication between developers in the United States and India. We set up a wiki and started a protocol where we would update the wiki every day, but I realized at some point that we were violating the DRY (Don't Repeat Yourself) principle, because we were putting the same comments in code check-ins and the wiki update. So, we wrote a little developer shim as a post-commit hook for Subversion. This little program listens for check-ins, automatically pulls the developer comments out, and posts them to the wiki. The wiki we're using (Instiki, http://instiki.org/) publishes RSS updates for Wiki updates. Now, on all our pairing workstations, we installed an RSS reader that launches automatically as part of our goodMorning task in Nant. This means that everyone who sits down to develop gets an update on all the stuff that has happened in the project since they last read the updates.

A.3 Andrew Glover

Favorite Technical Books

- *Java Design* [CMK98] by Peter Coad and others. ALthough this book seems ancient (it was written in 1998), Chapters 2 and 3 are probably the best reading out there because they cover designing with composition rather than inheritance and designing with interfaces. These two techniques, when applied correctly, separate the professional from the hobbyist.

- Bruce Eckel's *Thinking in Java* [Eck06] and Joshua Bloch's *Effective Java* [Blo01] are two classics that every Java developer should read cover to cover.

- I found *Software by Numbers* [DCH03] by Denne and Cleland-Huang quite interesting from a management standpoint.

Favorite Developer Tools

- Google's RSS reader has an intuitive aggregation platform that saves me from surfing a variety of sites for information.

- The WordPress blogging platform is incredibly simple to get up and running, and there is a rich community out there for support and new features.

A.4 Kirk Knoernschild

Favorite Technical Book

There are a lot of technical books that I reference frequently, but the most frequent must be *Design Patterns* [GHJV95].

Favorite Tools

I wouldn't say I have a favorite tool. It's really a genre of tools that helps me write better code. This includes tuff like JUnit, Emma, PMD, JDepend, JarAnalyzer, etc. They must be easy to use and light.

A.5 Mark Richards

Favorite Technical Books

- *Death March* [You99] by Edward Yourdon. Although things will never change, it is always good to know how and when you will run into the death spiral of IT projects. This book is a must for anyone involved in a large or difficult project.

- *Expert One-on-One J2EE Design and Development* [Joh02] by Rod Johnson. This book lays the foundation for the Spring framework and does a great job explaining when to use EJB and when not to use it. It is an excellent book and should be required reading for any J2EE architect or developer.

- My recent "fun" technical book is the Ted Nelson two-fer: *Dream Machines* and *Computer Lib* (1974). I recently was able to get my hands on this little gem from a friend of mine. What an amazing book. One side has *Dream Machines*; flip it over and you get *Computer Lib*. Although outdated, it is a classic and is fun to read.

Favorite Technical Tool

I have two answers to this question. First, I must say that the digital camera has recently become one of my favorite productivity tools. There is no better way of capturing a whiteboard design session better than with one of these little babies, especially when you are getting kicked out of a conference room! Second, from the software standpoint, I would have to say Eclipse. You can do anything with this tool—including end-user rich client GUIs. It is the wave of the future, and my prediction is that it will replace browser software within the next ten years.

A.6   Ian Roughley

Favorite Technical Books

Working Effectively with Legacy Code [Fea04] by Michael C. Feathers and *Object-Oriented Reengineering Patterns* [DDN02] by Serge Demeyer, Stéphane Ducasse, and Oscar Nierstrasz. These books provide a wealth of information in the form of strategies and solutions for not only working with legacy code but also working with code that you are not familiar with.

Favorite Technical Tool

Groovy. I find myself using Groovy more and more, especially now that IDE plug-ins are available (even though they are still immature). The feature I like the most is being able to utilize my existing Java code and libraries from within a scripting environment. Experimenting with code, writing tests, and quickly throwing together scripts for those one-off tasks has never been easier!

A.7   Brian Sletten

Favorite Technical Books

The Social Life of Information [BD02] by John Seely Brown and Paul Duguid and Bo Leuf's *The Semantic Web: Crafting Infrastructure for Agency* [Leu06]

Favorite Technical Discoveries

- NetKernel (http://www.1060.org) is a scalable platform that marries the best of REST and Unix pipelines for XML processing and other goodness.

- ActiveRDF (http://activerdf.m3pe.org/) is a Ruby library to create an Active Record–like way of dealing with RDF.

- Elmo (http://www.openrdf.org) is a library for dealing with several-well known SemWeb vocabularies in idiomatic Java.

- MINA,[1] Multipurpose Infrastructure for Network Application, a network application framework that is part of the Apache Directory Project. It supports the development of high-performance, highly scalable network applications.

---

[1] http://directory.apache.org/subprojects/mina/

A.8 Eitan Suez

Favorite Technical Books

On the technical front, it's *Agile Web Development with Rails* [TH05]. This sounds a little corny, but I have to hand it to Dave Thomas. I believe he has written what I consider to be one of the best books of the year, from the way the book is organized (comprehensive tutorial and comprehensive reference) to how completely thoroughly the book covers the technology it targets and finally to the revolutionary nature of the technology itself. It's a winner.

On the nontechnical front, I have recently read a relatively old book: *Night* [Wie82] by Elie Wiesel. I cannot think of another book that has made a stronger impression on me.

Favorite Developer Tools

I had a difficult time naming a single tool. Here are four; each is a favorite in its own category:

- Ubuntu Linux is a terrific environment that is composition of tools that has been a joy to discover and work with over the last nine months. It includes Gnome, apt-get, and the synaptic package manager, various GTK and Qt apps for everything from email (Evolution) to RSS readers (Straw), browsers (Epiphany), simple text editors (gedit), and much more.

- Markdown is the way writing for web publishing was meant to be. Its name says it all: Markdown is less markup; it frees writers from the chains/tedium of HTML authoring and allows them to concentrate on what they have to say. This is the way to more prolific writing and authoring for the Web.

- Typo CMS is a terrific, simple, extensible, Rails-based content management system. Although there are literally hundreds of content management systems to choose from these days, this one is a winner because it supports Markdown. It is Rails-based and so can be easily learned, understood, extended, and customized.

- IntelliJ IDEA is still a terrific, fast IDE for Java development and more. It has good support for XML editing, JavaScript, and CSS. It's nice to have it all under a single environment. It is still the workhorse for Java development.

A.9   Glenn Vanderburg

Favorite Technical Book

I just reread Tom DeMarco and Timothy Lister's *Waltzing with Bears: Managing Risk on Software Projects* [DL03]. Even though I read it just a few years ago, it was well worth reading again. It's full of truth, uncommon common sense, and excellent pragmatic advice for effective risk management (or, as the authors call it, "project management for grown-ups").

Favorite Developer Tool

My favorite recent discovery is a tool for Mac web developers called Xyle Scope, from Cultured Code. It's a fantastic tool for understanding and debugging web page formatting.

Appendix B

Resources

B.1 Bibliography

[BD02]   John Seely Brown and Paul Duguid. *The Social Life of Information*. Harvard Business School Press, 2002.

[Bec96]   Kent Beck. *Smalltalk Best Practice Patterns*. Prentice Hall, Englewood Cliffs, NJ, 1996.

[Bec00]   Kent Beck. *Extreme Programming Explained: Embrace Change*. Addison-Wesley, Reading, MA, 2000.

[Blo01]   Joshua Bloch. *Effective Java Programming Language Guide*. Addison Wesley Longman, Reading, MA, 2001.

[CMK98]   Peter Coad, Mark Mayfield, and Jonathan Kern. *ava Design: Building Better Apps and Applets*. Prentice Hall, Englewood Cliffs, NJ, 1998.

[Coc04]   Alistair Cockburn. *Crystal Clear: A Human-Powered Methodology for Small Teams*. Addison Wesley Longman, Reading, MA, 2004.

[Dav06]   Scott Davis. *Pragmatic GIS*. The Pragmatic Programmers, LLC, Raleigh, NC, and Dallas, TX, 2006.

[DCH03]   Mark Denne and Jane Cleland-Huang. *Software by Numbers: Low-Risk, High-Return Development*. Prentice Hall, Englewood Cliffs, NJ, 2003.

[DDN02]   Serge Demeyer, Stéğshane Ducasse, and Oscar Nierstrasz. *Object-Oriented Reengineering Patterns*. Morgan Kaufman, 2002.

[DL03]   Tom Demarco and Timothy Lister. *Waltzing with Bears: Managing Risk on Software Projects*. Dorset House, New York, NY, 2003.

[Eck06]   Bruce Eckel. *Thinking in Java*. Prentice Hall, Englewood Cliffs, NJ, fourth edition, 2006.

[Fea04]   Michael Feathers. *Working Effectively with Legacy Code*. Prentice Hall, Englewood Cliffs, NJ, 2004.

[For03]   Neal Ford. *Art of Java Web Development: Struts, Tapestry, Commons, Velocity, JUnit, Axis, Cocoon, InternetBeans, Web-Work*. Manning Publications Co., Greenwich, CT, 2003.

[FWA⁺99]   Neal Ford, Ed Weber, Talal Azzouka, Terry Dietzler, and Casey Williams. *JBuilder 3 Unleashed*. Sams Publishing, Indianapolis, IN, 1999.

[Gea99]   David Geary. *Graphic Java 2: Swing*. Prentice Hall, Englewood Cliffs, NJ, 1999.

[GH04]   David Geary and Cay Horstmann. *Core JavaServer Faces*. Prentice Hall, Englewood Cliffs, NJ, 2004.

[GHJV95]   Erich Gamma, Richard Helm, Ralph Johnson, and John Vlissides. *Design Patterns: Elements of Reusable Object-Oriented Software*. Addison-Wesley, Reading, MA, 1995.

[Gla02]   Malcolm Gladwell. *The Tipping Point: How Little Things Can Make a Big Difference*. Back Bay Books, 2002.

[Gra04]   Paul Graham. *Hackers and Painters: Big Ideas from the Computer Age*. O'Reilly & Associates, Inc, Sebastopol, CA, 2004.

[HM05]   Rob Harrop and Jan Machacek. *Pro Spring*. Apress, Berkeley, CA, 2005.

[III99]   James A. Highsmith III. *Adaptive Software Development: A Collaborative Approach to Managing Complex Systems*. Dorset House, New York, NY, 1999.

[Joh02]   Rod Johnson. *Expert One-on-One J2EE Design and Development*. Wrox, 2002.

[Kay03]   Doug Kaye. *Loosely Coupled: The Missing Pieces of Web Services*. RDS Press, 2003.

[Kno01]   Kirk Knoernschild. *Java Design: Objects, UML, and Process.* Pearson Education, Indianapolis, IN, 2001.

[Lad03]   Ramnivas Laddad. *AspectJ in Action: Practical Aspect-Oriented Programming.* Manning Publications Co., 2003.

[Lak96]   John Lakos. *Large-Scale C++ Software Design.* Addison Wesley Longman, Reading, MA, 1996.

[Lar04]   Craig Larman. *Agile and Iterative Development: A Manager's Guide.* Addison-Wesley, Reading, MA, 2004.

[LD05]   Steven D. Levitt and Stephen J. Dubner. *Freakonomics: A Rogue Economist Explores the Hidden Side of Everything.* William Morrow, 2005.

[Leu06]   Bo Leuf. *The Semantic Web: Crafting Infrastructure for Agency.* John Wiley & Sons, 2006.

[MD05]   Tom Marrs and Scott Davis. *JBoss at Work: A Practical Guide.* O'Reilly & Associates, Inc, Sebastopol, CA, 2005.

[MO05]   Vincent Massol and Timothy O'Brien. *Maven: A Developer's Notebook.* O'Reilly & Associates, Inc, Sebastopol, CA, 2005.

[PP03]   Mary Poppendieck and Tom Poppendieck. *Lean Software Development: An Agile Toolkit for Software Development Managers.* Addison-Wesley, Reading, MA, 2003.

[Ray03]   Eric S. Raymond. *The Art of UNIX Programming.* Addison-Wesley, Reading, MA, 2003.

[RG05]   Jared Richardson and Will Gwaltney. *Ship It! A Practical Guide to Successful Software Projects.* The Pragmatic Programmers, LLC, Raleigh, NC, and Dallas, TX, 2005.

[Sch04]   Ken Schwaber. *Agile Project Management with Scrum.* Microsoft Press, Redmond, WA, 2004.

[Sch05]   Barry Schwartz. *The Paradox of Choice: Why More Is Less.* Harper Perennial, 2005.

[Sub05]   Venkat Subramaniam. *.NET Gotchas.* O'Reilly & Associates, Inc, Sebastopol, CA, 2005.

[Sub06]   Venkat Subramaniam. *Practices of an Agile Developer: Working in the Real World.* The Pragmatic Programmers, LLC, Raleigh, NC, and Dallas, TX, 2006.

[TH05]   David Thomas and David Heinemeier Hansson. *Agile Web Development with Rails*. The Pragmatic Programmers, LLC, Raleigh, NC, and Dallas, TX, 2005.

[TYBG04]   Jon Thomas, Matthew Young, Kyle Brown, and Andrew Glover. *Java Testing Patterns*. Wiley, 2004.

[Wei02]   David Weinberger. *Small Pieces Loosely Joined: A Unified Theory of the Web*. Perseus Books Group, Cambridge, MA, 2002.

[WFW95]   Edward C. Weber, J. Neal Ford, and Christopher R. Weber. *Developing with Delphi: Object-Oriented Techniques*. Prentice Hall, Englewood Cliffs, NJ, 1995.

[Wie82]   Elie Wiesel. *Night*. Bantam, 1982.

[You99]   Edward Yourdon. *Death March: The Complete Software Developer's Guide to Surviving âĂŸMission Impossible' Projects*. Prentice Hall, Englewood Cliffs, NJ, 1999.

Index

Help for the Whole Team

Congratulations on joining the world-wide Pragmatic community. Together, we can make a difference to *developers* and their *managers* interested in a better way.

Here are some of our other Pragmatic Bookshelf titles that you and your team may enjoy.

Ship It!

This book shows you how to run a software project and *Ship It!*, on time and on budget, without excuses. You'll learn the common technical infrastructure that every project needs along with well-accepted, easy-to-adopt, best-of-breed practices that really work, as well as common problems and how to solve them.

Ship It!: A Practical Guide to Successful Software Projects
Jared Richardson and Will Gwaltney
200 pages. ISBN: 0-9745140-4-7

My Job Went to India

The job market is shifting. Your current job may be outsourced, perhaps to India or eastern Europe. But you can save your job and improve your career by following these practical and timely tips. See how to: • treat your career as a business • build your own personal brand • develop a structured plan for keeping your skills up to date • market yourself to your company and rest of the industry • keep your job!

**My Job Went to India:
52 Ways to Save Your Job**
Chad Fowler
230 pages. ISBN: 0-9766940-1-8

The Pragmatic Bookshelf

The Pragmatic Bookshelf features books written by working practitioners. The titles continue the well-known Pragmatic Programmer style, and continue to garner awards and rave reviews. As software development gets more and more difficult, the Pragmatic Programmers will be there with more titles and products to help programmers and their managers stay on top of their game.

Visit Us Online

No Fluff Just Stuff 2006
pragmaticprogrammer.com/titles/nfjs06
Web home for this book, where you can find and submit errata, send us feedback, and find other related resources.

Register for Updates
pragmaticprogrammer.com/updates
Be notified when updates and new books become available.

Join the Community
pragmaticprogrammer.com/community
Read our weblogs, join our online discussions, participate in our mailing list, interact with our wiki, and benefit from the experience of other Pragmatic Programmers.

New and Noteworthy
pragmaticprogrammer.com/news
Check out the latest pragmatic developments in the news.

Save on the PDF

Save on the PDF version of this book. Owning the paper version of this book entitles you to purchase the PDF version at a substantial discount. PDF is great for carrying around on your laptop. It's hyperlinked and is fully searchable. Buy it now at
pragmaticprogrammer.com/coupon

Contact Us

Phone Orders:	1-800-699-PROG (+1 919 847 3884)
Online Orders:	http://www.pragmaticprogrammer.com/catalog
Customer Service:	orders@pragmaticprogrammer.com
Non-English Versions:	translations@pragmaticprogrammer.com
Pragmatic Teaching:	academic@pragmaticprogrammer.com
Author Proposals:	proposals@pragmaticprogrammer.com